USDA

United States
Department of
Agriculture

Forest Service

**Northern
Research Station**

General Technical
Report NRS-P-31

Biofuels, Bioenergy, and Bioproducts from Sustainable Agricultural and Forest Crops

Proceedings of the Short Rotation Crops International Conference

Bloomington, Minnesota, USA
August 19-21, 2008

The Editors

Ronald S. Zalesny Jr. is Research Plant Geneticist, Northern Research Station, Institute for Applied Ecosystem Studies, 5985 Highway K, Rhinelander, WI 54501.

Rob Mitchell is Research Agronomist, U.S. Department of Agriculture, Agricultural Research Service, Grain, Forage, & Bioenergy Research Unit, 314 Biochemistry Hall, University of Nebraska-Lincoln, Lincoln, NE 68583.

Jim Richardson is Technical Director, Poplar Council of Canada, 1876 Saunderson Drive, Ottawa, ON, K1G 2C5, Canada.

Cover Photos

Front cover, clockwise from top left:

Poplar biomass crops in Quebec, Canada with pulp and paper processing facility in the background. Photo by Ron Zalesny, U.S. Forest Service.

Each round switchgrass bale in eastern Nebraska will yield about 50 gallons of ethanol. Photo by Rob Mitchell, USDA Agricultural Research Service.

Harvesting 3-year-old willow biomass crops in central New York using a Case New Holland forage harvester and a specially designed willow cutting head. Photo used with permission, Tim Volk, State University of New York.

Harvesting 4 tons of switchgrass per acre in late July in Nebraska. Photo by Rob Mitchell, USDA Agricultural Research Service.

Biofuels, Bioenergy, and Bioproducts from Sustainable Agricultural and Forest Crops

Proceedings of the Short Rotation Crops International Conference

Bloomington, Minnesota, USA
August 19-21, 2008

Edited by:
Ronald S. Zalesny, Jr., Rob Mitchell, and Jim Richardson

Published by:
U.S. Forest Service
Northern Research Station
Newtown Square, Pennsylvania

CONTENTS

Preface and Editors' Note vii
   Ronald S. Zalesny, Jr., Rob Mitchell, and Jim Richardson

Conference Organizers viii

Sponsoring Organizations ix

Development of a Willow Biomass Crop Harvester Based on a New Holland Forage
Harvester and Specially Designed Willow Cutting Head 1
   *Lawrence P. Abrahamson, Timothy A. Volk, Ed Priepke, John Posselius, Daniel J. Aneshansley,
   and Lawrence B. Smart*

25×'25: America's Energy Future 2
   R. Bruce Arnold

Pulling It All Together—Planning Guidelines and Design Tools for Creating
Multi-purpose Landscapes to Support Energy Objectives 3
   Gary Bentrup, Gary Wells, Michele Schoeneberger, and Michael Dosskey

Woody Biomass Crops in the Midwestern United States: Past, Present, and Future 4
   William E. Berguson

Water Perspectives on Large Scale Bioenergy 5
   Göran Berndes

Agroforest Management Systems can Produce Biofuel Feedstocks and Improve Key
Environmental Services on Retired Agricultural Lands in the Western Gulf Region 6
   Michael A. Blazier, Hal O. Liechty, Matthew H. Pelkki, Philip A. Tappe, and Charles P. West

Biofuels are Pest Food, Too! 7
   John J. Brown, R. Andrew Rodstrom, Eugene R. Hannon, Neal T. Kittelson, and Douglas B. Walsh

Economics of Willow Biomass Production and Policy to Enhance Market Penetration 8
   Thomas S. Buchholz, Timothy A. Volk, Michael J. Kelleher, and Lawrence P. Abrahamson

Coppice Culture for Biomass Production in Southeastern United States 9
   Mark Coleman and Douglas Aubrey

Swedish Experiences with Applications of Municipal and Industrial Residues on
Large-scale Short-rotation Coppice Plantations 10
   Ioannis Dimitriou and Pär Aronsson

Hybrid Aspen Growth Response to Shearing in Minnesota: Implications for
Biomass Production and Carbon Sequestration 11
   Grant M. Domke, Anthony W. D'Amato, Andrew J. David, and Alan R. Ek

Agroforestry and Cellulosic Ethanol from Sustainable Poplar Tree Farms 12
   Jake Eaton

Intensive Utilization of Harvest Residues in Southern Pine Plantations: Quantities
Available and Implications for Nutrient Budgets and Sustainable Site Productivity 13
   Mark H. Eisenbies, Eric D. Vance, W. Michael Aust, and John R. Seiler

Life-cycle Analysis of Small-scale Energy Systems Utilizing Oilseeds Grown in
the Midwest 14
   Seth Fore, Paul Porter, and William Lazarus

Use of Marginal Land and Water to Maximize Biofuel Production 15
  Gayathri Gopalakrishnan, M. Cristina Negri, Michael Wang, May Wu, and Seth Snyder

Sustainable Bioenergy Production in Agroforestry Systems 16
  Andrew Gordon, Dean Current, Michele Schoeneberger, and Gary Bentrup

Short-rotation Forestry in Germany: Lessons from the Past, Present Research
Activities, and Future Perspectives 17
  Holger Grünewald and Georg von Wühlisch

Woody Bioenergy Systems in the United States 18
  Richard B. Hall

The Council for Sustainable Biomass Production 19
  John Heissenbuttel

Effect of Landscape Positions and their Associated Soil and Terrain Attributes on
Biomass Crop Yield and Growth Rates 20
  *Gregg A. Johnson, Ryan T. Thelemann, Haowen Cai, Sudipto Banerjee, Craig C. Sheaffer,
  Hans-Joachim G. Jung, Katie B. Petersen, and Ulrike W. Tschirner*

Bioenergy: Agricultural Crop Residues 21
  Jane M.F. Johnson

Competition-induced Growth Increases in Poplar 22
  Jon D. Johnson and Jeff C. Kallestad

Evaluating Willow and Hybrid Poplar Clones for Biomass Volumes 23
  Allan Jurgens

Assessing Hybrid Poplar Biomass Feedstock Quality Using Near Infrared
Spectroscopy and Multivariate Data Analysis 24
  Jeff C. Kallestad and Jon D. Johnson

Rye in a Cellulosic Corn System 25
  Michael Kantar and Paul Porter

Conservation Management Strategies in Ethanol Crop Production:
A Brazil-U.S. Comparison 26
  Hazen Kazaks

Effects of a Winter Rye Double Crop after Corn Silage on Biomass Production,
Water Quality, and Soil Nutrient Status 27
  Erik Krueger, Tyson Ochsner, Paul Porter, Donald Reicosky, and John Baker

Important Developments for Short-rotation Intensive Culture of Willow in Different
Regions of Eastern Canada 28
  Michel Labrecque and Traian Ion Teodorescu

Environmental Services from Agroforest Systems: Sustainable Biofuel Feedstock
Production in the Gulf South Region of the United States 29
  Hal O. Liechty, Michael Blazier, Philip A. Tappe, and Matthew H. Pelkki

Using a Systems Approach to Improve Bioenergy Sustainability Assessment 30
  Valerie A. Luzadis, Timothy A. Volk, and Thomas S. Buchholz

Productivity and Energy Content of Native Perennial Grassland Species 31

Margaret E. Mangan, Craig C. Sheaffer, Donald L. Wyse, Peter H. Graham, Ulrike W. Tschirner, and Sanford Weisberg

Purpose-grown Trees as a Sustainable Renewable Energy Source 32

James Mann

R&D and Adoption Issues for Four Short-rotation Afforestation/Agroforestry Technologies: Results of Focus Groups Conducted in Quebec and the Canadian Prairies 33

Sylvain Masse and Pierre P. Marchand

A Minnesota-based *Populus* Breeding and Hybrid Poplar Development Program 34

Bernard G. McMahon, William E. Berguson, Daniel J. Buchman, Thomas E. Levar, Craig C. Maly, and Timothy C. O'Brien

Ecological Services Payments Enhance the Economies of Sustainably-grown Feedstocks 35

Linda Meschke

Growth and Yield of Poplar and Willow Hybrids in the Central Upper Peninsula of Michigan 36

Raymond O. Miller and Bradford A. Bender

Response of Three *Salix* Varieties to Irrigation with Different Concentrations of Solvay Storm Water 37

Jaconette Mirck and Timothy A. Volk

Biomass Production from Native Warm-season Grass Monocultures and Polycultures Managed for Bioenergy 38

Rob Mitchell and Kenneth Vogel

Herbaceous Biomass: State of the Art 39

Kenneth J. Moore

Use of Selected Hybrid Poplars in Short-rotation Woody Crops Production: The European Experience from the Field to the Final Transformer 40

Fabrizio Nardin and Franco Alasia

Prolonged Planting Season in Willow Short-rotation Forestry: Effects on Initial Plant Growth and Plant Survival 41

Nils-Erik Nordh, Pär Aronsson, and Theo Verwijst

Strategic Assessment of Biofuels Potential for the Western U.S. 42

Marcia Patton-Mallory, Richard Nelson, Ken Skog, Bryan Jenkins, Nathan Parker, Peter Tittmann, Quinn Hart, Ed Gray, Anneliese Schmidt, and Gayle Gordon

Impact of Growth Environment Variability on Alfalfa Yield, Cellulosic Ethanol Traits, and Paper Pulp Characteristics 43

Katie B. Petersen, Ryan T. Thelemann, Hans-Joachim G. Jung, Ulrike W. Tschirner, Craig C. Sheaffer, and Gregg A. Johnson

Characterization of Arsenic Uptake under Phosphorus Sufficient and Deficient Conditions in Shrub Willow (*Salix* spp.) Clones of Differing As Sensitivities 44

Emily E. Pulley and Lawrence B. Smart

Impacts of Paper Sludge, Manure, and Fertilizer Application on Soil Properties and Biomass Production in a Short Rotation Willow Cropping System in Central New York.....45
Amos K. Quaye, Timothy A. Volk, Sasha D. Hafner, Don J. Leopold, and Charles D. Schirmer

High Throughput Analysis Methods for Short-rotation Crops..46
Timothy G. Rials and Nicole Labbé

Sugar/Energy Canes as Feedstocks for the Biofuels Industry...47
Ed Richard, Jr., Thomas Tew, Robert Cobill, and Anna Hale

Production of Biomass for Energy from Sustainable Forestry Systems: Canada and Europe...48
Jim Richardson

Pacific Northwest Poplars: A Resilient Arthropod Community and the Distribution of Insect-caused Mortality in Cuttings...49
R. Andrew Rodstrom, John J. Brown, and John R. Rodstrom

Impacts of Biofuel Production on Grassland Birds in Wisconsin...50
David W. Sample and Christine A. Ribic

Challenges Associated with Short-rotation Biofuel Plantation Establishment in the Lower Mississippi Alluvial Valley...51
Jamie L. Schuler, Matthew H. Pelkki, and H. Christoph Stuhlinger

A National Assessment of Current and Future State of Technology for Woody Crops in Meeting Mandated Biofuel Requirements...52
Anna M. Shamey, Robert D. Perlack, and Lynn L. Wright

Wood-to-Wheels: A Multidisciplinary Research Initiative in Sustainable Transportation Utilizing Fuels and Co-products from Forest Resources.........................53
David R. Shonnard, Jeffrey D. Naber, Qiong Zhang, Ann L. Maclean, Kathleen E. Halvorsen, and John W. Sutherland

Genetics of Yield and Biomass Composition of Shrub Willow Bioenergy Crops Bred and Selected in North America...54
Lawrence B. Smart, Michelle J. Serapiglia, Kimberly D. Cameron, Arthur J. Stipanovic, Timothy A. Volk, and Lawrence P. Abrahamson

Socially Responsible Expansion of Brazilian Ethanol..55
Gerd Sparovek, Rodrigo Maule, and Göran Berndes

Genetic Improvement of Hybrid Poplar for the Renewable Fuels Industry: A Pacific Northwest Perspective...56
Brian J. Stanton, Jon D. Johnson, and David B. Neale

Irrigation Effects in a Cottonwood Plantation in the Lower Mississippi River Alluvial Valley..57
H. Christoph Stuhlinger, Paul F. Doruska, and Matthew H. Pelkki

Ecological Aspects of Cellulosic Biomass Supply from Whole-tree Chipping and Slash Removal...58
Philip A. Tappe, Matthew H. Pelkki, Robert L. Ficklin, and Hal O. Liechty

Canopy Structure, Light Interception, and Light-use Efficiency in Willow........................59
Pradeep J. Tharakan, Timothy A. Volk, Chris A. Nowak, and Godfrey J. Ofezu

Building a Cellulosic Biofuels Industry from the Ground Up: Tennessee Biofuels Initiative 60

Kelly Tiller

Poplar and Willow Short Rotation Intensive Culture (SRIC) Crops in Western Canada 61

Cees ("Case") van Oosten

Wood Bioenergy Systems in Canada 62

Ken C.J. Van Rees

Regional Site-selection Models for Hybrid Poplars 63

Robert C. Venette, Michael E. Ostry, and Kathleen M. Ward

Development of Switchgrass into a Biomass Energy Crop 64

Kenneth Vogel, Rob Mitchell, and Gautam Sarath

Illinois Studies of *Miscanthus* × *giganteus* for Biomass Feedstock Production 65

Tom Voigt

Commercializing Willow Biomass Crops for Bioenergy and Bioproducts in the Northeastern and Midwestern United States 66

Timothy A. Volk, Lawrence P. Abrahamson, Thomas E. Amidon, Daniel J. Aneshansley, Kimberly D. Cameron, Gregg A. =Johnson, John Posselius, Dennis Rak, Lawrence B. Smart, Eric Spomer, and Edwin H. White

Evaluating Effluent and Canal Water Irrigation for Wood Biomass Production and Phytotechnology 67

N. Larry White

A Comparative Cost Analysis of Logistics for Herbaceous Energy Crops and Short-rotation Woody Crops 68

Erin G. Wilkerson, Robert D. Perlack, and Anthony F. Turhollow

Multiple Criteria Deciding on Phytoremediation of a Heavy Metal Contaminated Agricultural Area Case: The Campine, Belgium 69

Nele Witters, Ann Ruttens, and Theo Thewys

***Populus* Root System Morphology During Phytoremediation of Landfill Leachate** 70

Jill A. Zalesny, Ronald S. Zalesny, Jr., David R. Coyle, Richard B. Hall, and Edmund O. Bauer

Potential Chloride and Sodium Uptake for 2- to 11-Year-Old *Populus* Irrigated with Landfill Leachate in the North Central United States 71

Jill A. Zalesny and Ronald S. Zalesny, Jr.

Biomass Potential of *Populus* in the Midwestern United States 72

Ronald S. Zalesny, Jr., Richard B. Hall, Jill A. Zalesny, William E. Berguson, Bernard G. McMahon, and Glen R. Stanosz

Variation in Lateral and Basal Adventitious Rooting of *Populus* Irrigated with Landfill Leachate: Selection of Favorable Genotypes for Environmental Benefits 73

Ronald S. Zalesny Jr. and Jill A. Zalesny

Evaluation of the Potential of Hybrid Willow as a Sustainable Biomass Energy Alternative Crop in Northern and West-Central Minnesota 74

Diomides Zamora, Dean Current, and Mike Demchik

Author Index 75

PREFACE AND EDITORS' NOTE

Ronald S. Zalesny, Jr., Rob Mitchell, and Jim Richardson

We are pleased to present the proceedings of the Short Rotation Crops International Conference: Biofuels, Bioenergy, and Bioproducts from Sustainable Agricultural and Forest Crops held in Bloomington, MN, in August 2008. For quite some time, there has been a substantial need for an international conference integrating biological and social aspects of producing both herbaceous and woody crops for biofuels, bioenergy, and bioproducts. Increasing energy prices worldwide have made alternative sources economically feasible in recent times. Our conference goal was to create an international forum to strengthen old collaborations and create new partnerships to attack some of the pressing issues facing the world's demand for energy. This collection of abstracts represents many of the extensive efforts under way to help understand these issues. We hope these proceedings may help to spark further conversations among scientists, academicians, regulators, and the general public. We encourage you to contact the authors to cultivate such discussions.

We were thankful to work with a productive team of conference organizers (page viii) representing the private and public sectors from a broad range of scientific disciplines. Sponsorship of the conference was phenomenal (page ix). The collective efforts of organizers and sponsors helped create a diverse and balanced program. We are also grateful to Neil Nelson, Tom Schmidt, and Jill Zalesny for reviewing earlier versions of this document, as well as Susan Wright, Rhonda Cobourn and the rest of the production services team who produced these proceedings with a seemingly impossible timeframe. Lastly, we thank the authors for their diligent efforts in preparing abstracts, presentations, and posters, as well as the conference participants for contributing to the networking potential and knowledge base of the overall experience.

CONFERENCE ORGANIZERS

Steering Committee:

Bryce Stokes, Co-Chair; Marilyn Buford, Co-Chair; Michael Abbey, Andrew Arends, Tom Baumann, Bill Berguson, Michael Casler, Craig Cox, Dean Current, Rick Dahlman, Michael Demchik, Fred Deneke, Mark Downing, Jake Eaton, Alan Ek, Robert Escheman, Robert Fireovid, William Goldner, Andrew Gordon, Rick Hall, John Heissenbuttel, Dick Hemmingsen, Richard Hess, Keith Jacobson, Gregg Johnson, RaeLynn Jones-Loss, Hans Jung, Andrew Mason, Rob Mitchell, Jennifer Nguyen, Nathan Ramsey, Tim Rials, Jim Richardson, Michele Schoeneberger, Steve Shafer, Timothy Volk, Steve Yaddof, Mike Young, Jill Zalesny, Ronald Zalesny, Jr.

Registration:

RaeLynn Jones-Loss, Chair; Dean Current, Alan Ek, Jennifer Nguyen

Website:

RaeLynn Jones-Loss, Chair; Dean Current, Alan Ek, Sarah Finley, Jennifer Nguyen

Technical Program & Proceedings:

Rob Mitchell, Co-Chair; Ronald Zalesny, Jr., Co-Chair; Jim Richardson

Field Tours:

Bill Berguson, Co-Chair; Rick Hall, Co-Chair; Gregg Johnson, Hans Jung, Mike Young

Posters:

Jill Zalesny

SPONSORING ORGANIZATIONS

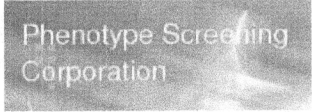

DEVELOPMENT OF A WILLOW BIOMASS CROP HARVESTER BASED ON A NEW HOLLAND FORAGE HARVESTER AND SPECIALLY DESIGNED WILLOW CUTTING HEAD

Lawrence P. Abrahamson[a],*, Timothy A. Volk[a], Ed Priepke[b], John Posselius[b], Daniel J. Aneshansley[c], and Lawrence B. Smart[a]

[a]College of Environmental Science and Forestry, State University of New York
[b]Case New Holland
[c]Department of Biological and Environmental Engineering, Cornell University

Willow shrubs have several characteristics that make them an ideal feedstock for biofuels, bioproducts, and bioenergy. They have been tested across the northeast and midwest United States and in Canada from Prince Edward Island to Alberta. The largest single cost factor for willow biomass crops is harvesting and transportation, which can account for up to 60 percent of the delivered cost of the biomass. The development of a cost-effective harvesting system that produces consistent sized chips has been a barrier to the deployment of willow biomass crops. SUNY's College of Environmental Science and Forestry has been working with Case New Holland and Cornell University for several years to develop an effective harvester system based on an FX-series New Holland forage harvester. A specially designed hydraulic driven willow cutting head manufactured by Coppice Resources Ltd. (CRL) in the United Kingdom has been fitted to the forage harvester for harvesting willow biomass crops. The FX45 forage harvester and modified cutting head were used during summer and winter of 2006. This combination was able to harvest 1.9-2.5 acres/hour with 70 percent field efficiency if stems were <3 inches in diameter and fairly uniform. Case New Holland fitted the CRL willow cutting head to a new FR-series forage harvester during fall of 2007 and after running trials they found that this series of forage harvester will be a more effective harvesting system than the previous FX forage harvesters. In limited trials (2007) with the FR forage harvester, harvesting rates of 3.6 acres/hour were reached. A forage blower was used to automatically unload a field forage wagon of willow chips into a chip trailer for road transport. Since fall of 2006 this method of transferring and transporting harvested chips has worked very successfully. The development of this willow harvesting system is helping to overcome barriers to the commercialization of willow biomass crops.

KEY WORDS: SRWC, biomass crops, willow cutting head, forage harvester

*Corresponding author: State University of New York, College of Environmental Science and Forestry, 224 Illick Hall, 1 Forestry Drive, Syracuse, NY 13210; Phone: (315) 470-6777; Email: labrahamson@esf.edu

25×'25: AMERICA'S ENERGY FUTURE

R. Bruce Arnold

Member: National Steering Committee of 25×'25

"25×'25: America's Energy Future" is a coalition of some 700 partners with diverse interests. Groups such as corporations; environmental organizations; farm and forest groups; religious organizations; and government, academic and Native American groups are among the partners in this organization. Twenty-nine U.S. governors have given their support, and 13 state legislatures have passed 25×'25 resolutions. The mission of 25×'25 is: "By 2025, America's farms, forests, and ranches will provide 25 percent of the total energy consumed in the United States while continuing to produce safe, abundant, and affordable food, feed, and fiber." This paper will discuss the partner-approved 25×'25 action plan to move the nation forward to attainment of the stated mission.

KEY WORDS: biomass, energy, action plan

*Contact information: 244 Wencin Terrace, West Chester, PA 19382-1990; Phone: (610) 431-6326; Email: brucearnld@aol.com

PULLING IT ALL TOGETHER—PLANNING GUIDELINES AND DESIGN TOOLS FOR CREATING MULTI-PURPOSE LANDSCAPES TO SUPPORT ENERGY OBJECTIVES

Gary Bentrup[a,*], Gary Wells[b], Michele Schoeneberger[a], and Michael Dosskey[b]

[a]USDA National Agroforestry Center, Forest Service, Southern Research Station
[b]USDA National Agroforestry Center, Natural Resources Conservation Service

Sustainable bioenergy production requires we plan, design, and manage lands across multiple scales and land uses, balancing energy production with the other services we want from these lands. This is a challenge on private lands, where action is controlled predominantly at the landowner level. "Pulling it all together" implies creating policies, programs, planning concepts, and design tools that take into account these many services so they can be implemented in concert rather than in conflict with each other. Planning guidelines are needed that better match land-use management to land capability, building in greater resiliency and flexibility on the land to future economic and climate vagaries. Tools also must be available for communicating and building support for multi-purpose landscapes. A conceptualized watershed supporting a diversified bioenergy platform, as well as production of food, feed, livestock, and environmental and social services, is presented. Productive conservation systems, especially agroforestry, are an integral part of this watershed. Actual planning and design of such a watershed requires a multi-scale planning framework and tools, such as those we have been developing at National Agroforestry Center. The Conservation Buffers Guidelines book, synthesized from 1,400+ research publications, provides illustrated rules-of-thumb for planning and designing buffers to address multiple objectives, including feedstock production and added conservation to mitigate bioenergy production impacts. A number of GIS-based suitability assessments (e.g. buffer performance and water quality, agroforestry products, riparian connectivity, and farming suitability) can be overlaid to provide guidance for optimally locating systems to meet multiple purposes. Other tools include a buffer-width tool for water quality and a cost-benefit analysis tool for then designing the individual practices in a system. CanVis provides photo-realistic scenarios that enable landowners to "test-drive" alternatives on the lands. By "Pulling it all together," landowners, natural resource professionals, communities and industry can build a sustainable, multi-purpose bioenergy future.

KEY WORDS: agroforestry, bioenergy, riparian forest buffers, planning, design

*Corresponding author: USDA FS/NRCS National Agroforestry Center, East Campus-University of Nebraska-Lincoln, Lincoln, NE 68583-0822; Phone: (402) 437-5178, ext. 4018; Email: gbentrup@fs.fed.us

WOODY BIOMASS CROPS IN THE MIDWESTERN UNITED STATES: PAST, PRESENT, AND FUTURE

William E. Berguson

Natural Resources Research Institute, University of Minnesota – Duluth

Hybrid poplar research has a long history in the Midwest beginning with the pioneering work of Dave Dawson at the U.S. Forestry Sciences Laboratory in Rhinelander, Wisconsin, in the 1970s. Since that time, research has been under way by a number of organizations throughout the region, including the US Forest Service, Iowa State, and the University of Minnesota. This foundation of existing research in the region eventually led to the commercial application of hybrid poplar plantations to supply fiber to a paper mill in central Minnesota. A plantation program was started in 1995 by Champion International and is being managed by Verso Paper, the current owner of the mill at Sartell, Minnesota. This project consists of more than 23,000 acres at this time. Research in poplar culture and genetic improvement accelerated in Minnesota with the formation of the Minnesota Hybrid Poplar Research Cooperative in 1996, which has carried out an aggressive program of breeding and field testing on Verso Paper property as well as other sites throughout Minnesota. Results of yield tests in commercially managed stands indicate that yields of current poplar clones can be expected to range from a minimum of 3.5 tons ac^{-1} yr^{-1} to 5.5 tons ac^{-1} yr^{-1}. Large-scale genetics field tests show promise for improvement of yield in the future with superior clones oftentimes exhibiting yields of 1.5 to 2.0 times that of current commercial hybrids. The history of poplar research and commercial application will be presented along with a discussion of current activities and needs for the future.

KEY WORDS: hybrid poplar, tree improvement, productivity, breeding

*Contact information: 5013 Miller Trunk Highway, Duluth, MN 55811; Phone: (218) 720-4296; Email: bberguso@nrri.umn.edu

*** INVITED SPEAKER ***

WATER PERSPECTIVES ON LARGE SCALE BIOENERGY

Göran Berndes

Chalmers University of Technology, Sweden

Long-term climate change is a growing challenge that will change the availability of land and water resources and also the pattern of biomass production. Furthermore, the adaptation and mitigation response strategies implemented by society can strongly influence land and water use: a growing global demand for both food and bioenergy is increasing the pressure on land and water resources, with implications for their ability to provide ecosystem support functions. The recent period of increasing food prices and land use changes in various parts of the world can be explained partly by the increasing bioenergy demand but also by rapid economic growth and changing food consumption patterns.

The presentation will review global and regional trends as well as longer-term scenarios for food and bioenergy, primarily based on a water perspective. Implications for water availability and use will be discussed with some global/regional conclusions. Stressing that the envisaged bioenergy development also implies opportunities, the presentation will further discuss the possibility of integrating the cultivation of new types of bioenergy crops within expanded agricultural systems in a modified water resource context. In the presenter's view, this is an area that has received too little attention in the present bioenergy debate. The use of bioenergy for mitigating climate change has been widely discussed but the role of bioenergy in agricultural strategies to adapt to climate change is less explored.

KEY WORDS: water demand, water resources, bioenergy, competition, synergies

*Contact information: Department of Energy and the Environment, Division of Physical Resource Theory, Chalmers University of Technology, Sweden; Phone: +46 31 772 3148; Email: goran.berndes@chalmers.se

*** INVITED SPEAKER ***

AGROFOREST MANAGEMENT SYSTEMS CAN PRODUCE BIOFUEL FEEDSTOCKS AND IMPROVE KEY ENVIRONMENTAL SERVICES ON RETIRED AGRICULTURAL LANDS IN THE WESTERN GULF REGION

Michael A. Blazier[a,*], Hal O. Liechty[b], Matthew H. Pelkki[b], Philip A. Tappe[b], and Charles P. West[c]

[a]*Louisiana State University AgCenter*
[b]*School of Forest Resources, University of Arkansas-Monticello*
[c]*Crop, Soil, and Environmental Sciences, University of Arkansas-Fayetteville*

To meet federal and state biofuel mandates in the United States, production of crops used as biofuel feedstocks must dramatically increase. Increasing biofuel production capacity will necessitate bolstering biofuel production from corn and soybean in the Midwest with crops grown in other regions of the country and with crops other than those conventionally used as biofuel feedstocks. However, dramatic expansion of lands used for agriculture could degrade environmental quality. Clearing forests reduces carbon sequestration and alters wildlife habitat. Increased fertilizer use associated with agriculture can lead to nutrient pollution of waterways. Agroforest management systems in which crops are harvested annually as biofuel feedstocks are grown in alleys between trees and can be used to enhance wildlife habitat and carbon sequestration of forests while producing biofuels. These systems have relatively low water and fertilizer requirements due to efficient allocation of growing space and site resources. Agroforest systems diversify farm markets and reduce economic risks of entering the biofuel market. Agroforest systems also provide key ecosystem services, such as increased carbon sequestration, reduced nitrogen pollution of waterways, and increased wildlife diversity. Fertilizer use could be further minimized by using such systems to produce switchgrass, a nutrient-efficient perennial grass with high biomass growth potential, as a biofuel feedstock. The Western Gulf region of the United States has abundant land that has been retired from agricultural and pastoral production due to changing economic or social trends. Producing biofuels on such lands with agroforest systems can enhance environmental services currently provided by such lands while increasing regional biofuel production. The information presented will discuss: (1) designs of these ecosystems, with concerns related to establishment, production, and harvesting; (2) likely impacts on soil and water quality and carbon sequestration; and (3) the potential influence of these systems on biodiversity in the Western Gulf region.

KEY WORDS: agroforestry, switchgrass, cottonwood, pine, biodiversity, nutrient cycling

*Corresponding author: Louisiana State University AgCenter Hill Farm Research Station, 11959 Highway 9, Homer, LA 71040; Phone: (318) 927-2578; Fax: (318) 927-9505; Cell: (318) 927-7671; Email: MBlazier@agcenter.lsu.edu

BIOFUELS ARE PEST FOOD, TOO!

John J. Brown*, R. Andrew Rodstrom, Eugene R. Hannon, Neal T. Kittelson,
and Douglas B. Walsh

Washington State University

Biofuel crops are monocultures that insects and diseases will use as an energy resource and they will compete with our intended use of these crops. Repeated land use for one cropping system without rotating crops will increase the potential for losses due to pest activities, and pest management will reduce profits. Site preparation to minimize pest populations will be rewarded. Irrigated cropping systems will facilitate delivery of pest control chemicals. What are the most serious pest problems in biofuel production? How can these pests be controlled? What is the cost/benefit ratio of control measures and what are the factors that define an economic threshold for initiation of control efforts? Many riparian species of insects attack both willow (*Salix*) and poplar (*Populus*) hosts. We have successfully used a synthetic sex pheromone to control a clearwing moth (Sessidae: *Paranthrene robiniae*) that can cause major damage to irrigated hybrid poplar grown in eastern Oregon and eastern Washington. Our efforts toward reducing populations of a carpenterworm moth (Cossidae: *Prionoxystus robiniae*) below an economic threshold show promise. Our most difficult pest problem in hybrid poplars is the poplar/willow borer (Curculionidae: *Cryptorhynchus lapathi*), which, true to its common name, attacks *Salix*, too. Repeated use of imidacloprid delivered through the dip system controls aphids (Chaitophorus: *Chaitophorus populicola*) and cottonwood leaf beetles (Chrysomelidae: *Chrysomela scripta*), and seems to be reducing the poplar/willow borer, too. Likewise, insect pests of corn, sugarcane, and rice are known to feed on *Miscanthus spp.*, and nematode and diseases of *Panicum virgatum* can severely reduce biomass production. Introduction of *Miscanthus* × *giganteus* has potential as a biofuel, but it could serve as an alternate host to corn (*Ostrinia nubilalis* and *Diatraea grandiosella*) and sugarcane pests (*Diatraea saccharalis*). With the potential of pest movement between crops a "Good Neighbor" pest control strategy may be required.

KEY WORDS: poplar, borers, pest control, sex pheromone, imidacloprid

*Corresponding author: Department of Entomology, Washington State University, Pullman, WA 99164-6382; Email: brownjj@wsu.edu; Phone: (509) 335-8089

ECONOMICS OF WILLOW BIOMASS PRODUCTION AND POLICY TO ENHANCE MARKET PENETRATION

Thomas S. Buchholz[a], Timothy A. Volk[a], Michael J. Kelleher[b],*,
and Lawrence P. Abrahamson[a]

[a]College of Environmental Sciences and Forestry, State University of New York (SUNY),
[b]SUNY Center for Sustainable and Renewable Energy

Woody biomass has significant potential as a sustainable energy source to provide society with fuel, thermal energy, and electrical power. Short-rotation coppice (SRC) willow crops are a promising source of biomass for the production of sustainable energy and bioproducts. However, current markets for biomass are thinly traded, the economics of willow plantations is little understood, and there are potential market barriers to the adoption of willow as a biomass energy crop. We analyze how financial incentives influence profitability of SRC willow plantations in upstate New York and identify barriers to further expansion. We introduce SRC willow plantation economics under different parameters that can impact market penetration, such as biomass productivity, land rent, biomass price, fuel costs, and labor costs. We then examine the impact of various incentives on profitability of SRC willow plantations. Financial incentives used include low-cost loans, annual subsidy payments, and establishment grants. We also examine the influence of nonfinancial factors, such as imperfect information, status quo bias, and land-ownership patterns, on the adoption of willow as a biomass energy crop.

Recent studies suggest that a 20-acre SRC willow plantation is economically viable only with a biomass productivity above 3 oven-dried-tons (odt)/acre/year and a biomass price of above \$50/odt. Dependence on start-up loans can obliterate a plantation's profitability.

We introduce various incentive scenarios using a mix of the three financial tools. Establishment grants are one of the most promising financial tools; a grant for 50 percent of establishment costs, or \$549/ acre, would nearly double the internal rate of return in the case study. Results indicate that incentives focusing on the early stages of plantation establishment are the most promising ones. We also develop policy recommendations to address the nonfinancial market—structural and ownership parameters that may impact SRC willow acreage expansion.

KEY WORDS: short-rotation coppice, willow crops, economic analysis, policy, incentive, market barriers

*Corresponding author: State University of New York, College of Environmental Science and Forestry, Department of Forest and Natural Resource Management, 220 Bray Hall, 1 Forestry Drive, Syracuse, NY 13210; Phone: (315) 470-4934; Email: mkellehe@esf.edu

COPPICE CULTURE FOR BIOMASS PRODUCTION IN SOUTHEASTERN UNITED STATES

Mark Coleman* and Douglas Aubrey

U.S. Forest Service, Southern Research Station, Savannah River

Coppice culture of hardwood trees is common in cool climates using willow, and in tropical regions using eucalyptus. However, coppice culture is rare in the southeastern United States, despite Klaus Steinbeck's successful applications using American sycamore (*Platanus occidentalis*) three decades ago. Sycamore, poplar, willow, and eucalyptus are candidate species for coppice culture in the southeastern United States. Southern latitude willow varieties are undomesticated, yet widespread distribution of the native *Salix nigra* indicates development potential. Sycamore's rapid early growth is a great advantage during coppicing. However, sycamore has been discounted as a biomass producing crop because dieback inevitably occurs during years 3 to 6. Coppicing sycamore may avoid disease establishment. Similarly, eucalyptus is easily killed aboveground by winter frosts in temperate climates, but roots are rarely damaged. Annual removal of frost-damaged eucalyptus tops would allow regrowth from protected rootstock. To collect information on biomass production and regrowth capacity for southeastern coppice culture, high-density test plots were installed at the Savannah River Site, near Aiken, SC. Plots were designed to include two hybrid poplar clones (OP-367, 15-29, *Eucalyptus grandis*, *E. amplifolia*), sycamore seedlings, and locally collected *Salix nigra*. Trees were planted at 14,815 trees ha^{-1} arranged in dual-row plantings developed for willow coppice culture. During the establishment year, sycamore and poplar clone OP-367 were top producers (3.4 ± 1.1 and 2.1 ± 0.9 Mg ha^{-1}, respectively). Stock quality negatively impacted willow and poplar clone 15-29 productivity (0.5 ± 0.2 and 0.8 ± 0.3 Mg ha^{-1}, respectively). We could not plant eucalyptus because of non-native planting restrictions at the Savannah River Site. However, frost damage and regrowth information collected for unmulched, styroblock-held seedlings indicates that survival and regrowth potential was greatest for *E. amplifolia*. Few *E. grandis* survived the 469 freezing hours that occurred, while most of the E. amplifolia survived with vigorous regrowth, thus demonstrating potential for coppice as a frost-avoidance biomass culture method.

KEY WORDS: sycamore, eucalyptus, willow, hybrid poplar, short-rotation woody crop, frost damage

*Corresponding author: Savannah River Forestry Sciences Lab, 241 Gateway Dr., Aiken, SC 29803; Phone: (803) 652-3632; Email: coleman.m@earthlink.net

SWEDISH EXPERIENCES WITH APPLICATIONS OF MUNICIPAL AND INDUSTRIAL RESIDUES ON LARGE-SCALE SHORT-ROTATION COPPICE PLANTATIONS

Ioannis Dimitriou* and Pär Aronsson

Swedish University of Agricultural Sciences

Short-rotation coppice (SRC) with willow (*Salix sp.*) is a commercial crop in Sweden grown on approximately 15,000 hectares of agricultural land to produce biomass for energy. The produced biomass is almost entirely used in district heating plants for combined heat and power generation. In recent years, nutrient-rich residues, mainly municipal and industrial wastewaters as landfill leachate and log-yard runoff, as well as solid material as sewage sludge and wood-ash, have been successfully applied to willow SRC to reduce fertilisation costs and simultaneously increase biomass production and/or facilitate alternative low-cost treatments. Pollutant and nutrient contents in residues and soils are reduced through plant uptake and microbial degradation, and at the same time biomass production is enhanced. The information provided will describe operating systems in Sweden where large-scale willow SRC plantations treat different residues (municipal wastewater, landfill leachate, log-yard runoff, sewage sludge, wood-ash) and simultaneously produce biomass. This presentation also will give results from research efforts to estimate parameters of special environmental concern (e.g., nutrient leaching, plant stress tolerance, heavy metal fluxes) related to such applications, in an effort to evaluate the risk of environmental hazards from such practices.

KEY WORDS: willow, *Salix*, Sweden, phytoremediation, vegetation filters, municipal wastewater, landfill leachate, log-yard runoff, sewage sludge, wood-ash

*Corresponding author: Swedish University of Agricultural Sciences, Department of Crop Production Ecology, Box 7043, 75007, Uppsala, Sweden. Phone: +46 18 672553; Email: ioannis.dimitriou@vpe.slu.se

HYBRID ASPEN GROWTH RESPONSE TO SHEARING IN MINNESOTA: IMPLICATIONS FOR BIOMASS PRODUCTION AND CARBON SEQUESTRATION

Grant M. Domke*, Anthony W. D'Amato, Andrew J. David, and Alan R. Ek

Department of Forest Resources, University of Minnesota,

Recent interest in the use of woody biomass for energy has created an opportunity for the development of silvicultural systems that can produce high levels of biomass over shorter rotations than traditional approaches to plantation management. One area within this arena where there is a great deal of potential is the management of short-rotation hybrid aspen. In particular, early successional hardwood tree species, such as those in the *Populus* genus, typically exhibit rapid initial height and diameter growth, making these species ideally suited for short-rotation forestry applications aimed at maximizing biomass production over short time scales. In many cases, greater levels of early growth have been achieved through the use of aspen hybrids (*Populus tremuloides* Michx. × *P. tremula* L.), which are crosses between quaking aspen (*P. tremuloides*) and European aspen (*P. tremula*). In addition to the rapid growth of these hybrids, the prolific root sprouting ability of this species presents potential management options for the production of woody biomass using coppice methods after initial plantation establishment. Moreover, the use of existing aspen root stocks as sources of regeneration for subsequent rotations provides a silviculturally straightforward and cost-effective means for sustaining these systems over multiple short rotations. Finally, the expansion of aspen root systems with each subsequent rotation provides a long-term opportunity for increasing belowground carbon storage on these sites. Here we present the results of a 15-year study investigating the growth response of hybrid aspen clones to shearing on upland sites in northern Minnesota. We describe specific clonal responses in terms of sucker density and early diameter and height growth. In addition, we use these findings to evaluate potential silvicultural options for managing these systems and their implications for carbon storage and biomass production for energy.

KEY WORDS: hybrid aspen, *Populus*, carbon sequestration, biomass production, growth and yield

*Corresponding author: University of Minnesota, Department of Forest Resources, 1530 Cleveland Ave. N., St. Paul, MN 55108; Phone: (612) 624-2202; Email: gmdomke@umn.edu

AGROFORESTRY AND CELLULOSIC ETHANOL FROM SUSTAINABLE POPLAR TREE FARMS

Jake Eaton

GreenWood Resources, Inc.

GreenWood Resources (GWR) manages 14,000 hectares of poplar farms in the Pacific Northwest region of the United States and is developing nurseries and short-rotation high-yield poplar plantations in Chile and China. The U.S. farms are managed on 12- to 15-year rotations for multiple products, including sawlogs, chips, and residuals for bioenergy. GWR intends to certify all the tree farms to the Forest Stewardship Council standard. In addition to the sawlog production business, GreenWood Resources is fully committed to the goal of developing renewable sources of energy. To this end, GreenWood is refining agronomic technologies that will optimize the production systems for poplar energy farms. Poplar feedstock will be used for cogeneration and pellet production, and it will become a feedstock of choice for cellulosic ethanol. Over the next 3 to 5 years it is GWR's goal to lead the development of sustainable poplar energy plantations in North America, South America, and China. GreenWood is well positioned to play a valuable role in bringing all of the essential elements together for successful commercialization of poplar tree farms for renewable energy. GWR is a global leader in the development of elite poplar germplasm as well as the production systems to optimize poplar energy farm operation. GWR has relationships with technology partners who will build pilot-scale cellulosic ethanol facilities that use poplar feedstock. Additionally the company has the ability to develop sound financial structures to access the capital that is required for large-scale project financing. The time is right for biomass energy to become a significant part of our future energy security. However, unprecedented investment will be required for biomass energy to become a reality. Questions related to sustainability and land use also will need to be addressed.

KEY WORDS: poplar, tree improvement, production systems, cellulosic ethanol, sustainability

*Contact information: GreenWood Resources, One World Trade Center, 121 SW Salmon St. Suite 1020, Portland, OR 97204; Phone: (971) 533-7056; Email: jake.eaton@gwrglobal.com

*** INVITED SPEAKER ***

INTENSIVE UTILIZATION OF HARVEST RESIDUES IN SOUTHERN PINE PLANTATIONS: QUANTITIES AVAILABLE AND IMPLICATIONS FOR NUTRIENT BUDGETS AND SUSTAINABLE SITE PRODUCTIVITY

Mark H. Eisenbies[a,*], Eric D. Vance[b], W. Michael Aust[c], and John R. Seiler[c]

[a]*U.S. Forest Service*
[b]*National Council for Air and Stream Improvement Incorporated*
[c]*Virginia Tech Department of Forestry*

The rising costs and social concerns over the use of fossil fuels have resulted in increased interest in and opportunities for biofuels. Biomass in the form of coarse woody residues left on site following traditional timber harvest in the southeastern United States constitutes a potentially significant source of biomass that could be utilized for bioenergy. Questions remain regarding whether the removal of this material would be a sustainable silvicultural practice given the potential impact on soil nutrient cycling and other ecosystem functions. Our objective is to use published studies to estimate quantities of residual materials that may be available as a source of bioenergy or biomaterials following harvest of southern pine forests. Quantities of nutrients potentially removed with the residues and their potential replacement with fertilizer are calculated, and a more general assessment of the implications of residue removals on sustainable productivity across a range of sites conducted. Generally between 50 and 80 Mg/ha of material are left on site after typical stem-only harvests, of which half could be removed using chippers at the landing. Based on these estimates, increase in mid-rotation fertilization rates of 45 to 60 percent may be needed on some sites to fully replace the nutrients removed for bioenergy. Field experiments show that residue removals do not degrade forest productivity in many cases, but more data are needed to assess the effects of frequent removals (i.e., from short-rotation systems) over long time periods and to identify sites that may be particularly sensitive to the practice. Markets for previously nonmerchantable materials also may provide incentives for improved forest management by landowners.

KEY WORDS: fertilization, forest soils, harvesting residues, sustainability

*Corresponding author: U.S. Forest Service, Box 9681, Mississippi State, MS 39759; Phone: (662) 325-8983; Email: meisenbies@fs.fed.us

LIFE-CYCLE ANALYSIS OF SMALL-SCALE ENERGY SYSTEMS UTILIZING OILSEEDS GROWN IN THE MIDWEST

Seth Fore*, Paul Porter, and William Lazarus

University of Minnesota

As the concern over price and supply of petroleum continues to increase, there are burgeoning efforts to find alternative sources of renewable fuel. Oilseeds commonly grown in the Midwest can be crushed on-farm to create vegetable oil and meal that can be utilized in numerous ways to decrease producers' demand for petroleum and feed products. Vegetable oil can be converted to biodiesel, run straight in diesel engines, or used as a heating fuel. The meal counterpart can be used a high-value protein substitute in livestock rations or can be burned in pellet stoves for heat generation. As alternative methods for producing renewable fuels emerge, it is important that complete life-cycle accounting measures are implemented to ensure there is a positive net energy balance over the petroleum product replaced. There is a need to conduct life-cycle analysis on small scale on-farm oilseed crushing systems to substantiate whether there is a positive net energy balance gained through utilizing oilseed crops grown on-farm as a replacement for fuel and feed.

KEY WORDS: small-scale energy production, life-cycle analysis, biodiesel, straight vegetable oil

*Corresponding author: University of Minnesota, Department of Agronomy and Plant Genetics, 1991 Upper Buford Circle, St. Paul, MN 55108; Phone: (701) 212-6625; Email: fore0046@umn.edu

USE OF MARGINAL LAND AND WATER TO MAXIMIZE BIOFUEL PRODUCTION

Gayathri Gopalakrishnan, M. Cristina Negri*, Michael Wang, May Wu, and Seth Snyder

Argonne National Laboratory, Energy Systems Division

The development of sustainable, renewable energy sources has become an issue of increasing importance due to both the recent increase in gasoline prices in the United States and the international scientific consensus to reduce greenhouse gas emissions to mitigate climate change. Advanced biofuels are a primary component of the emerging energy portfolio. To strengthen the nation's energy security, mitigate greenhouse gas emission, and revitalize the rural economy, the Energy Independence Security Act of 2007 mandated the production of 36 billion gallons of biofuels by 2022, of which 21 billion gallons must be advanced biofuels. This mandate would result in an increase in biomass production of approximately seven times the current amount—from 190 million dry tons to 1.36 billion dry tons of biomass. Biomass is a land-based renewable resource and such a significant increase is likely to result in large-scale conversion of land, from current uses to energy feedstock generation, potentially causing increases in the prices of food, land, and agricultural commodities as well as disruption of ecosystems. Further, while a majority of current bioenergy crops are not irrigated, their yield is usually dependent on water availability. This study evaluates sustainable production of bioenergy crops through the use of marginal land and impaired water and discusses the potential for growing cellulosic biofuel crops such as poplar and switchgrass in optimized systems such that (1) marginal land is brought into productive use; (2) impaired water is used to boost yields; (3) clean freshwater is left for other uses that require higher water quality; and (4) feedstock diversification is achieved that helps ecological sustainability, biodiversity, and economic opportunities for farmers.

KEY WORDS: cellulosic biomass, biofuels, marginal land, poplar, sustainability, water

*Corresponding author: Argonne National Laboratory, Energy Systems Division, Building 362 E-333, 9700 S. Cass Avenue, Argonne, IL; Phone: (630) 252-9662; Email: negri@anl.gov

SUSTAINABLE BIOENERGY PRODUCTION IN AGROFORESTRY SYSTEMS

Andrew M. Gordon[a,*], Dean Current[b], Michele Schoeneberger[c], and Gary Bentrup[c]

[a]Department of Environmental Biology, University of Guelph, Canada
[b]Center for Integrated Natural Resources and Agricultural Management, University of Minnesota
[c]National Agroforestry Center, Southern Research Station, U.S. Forest Service

The objective of this conference is to foster greater exchange between the agricultural and forestry sectors on the science and application of producing crops for biofuels, bioenergy, and bioproducts. However, the real challenge and opportunity lies in how agricultural and forestry efforts can actually be integrated to sustainably meet the future renewable energy targets facing the United States and the world. Agroforestry is just that—the combination of agricultural and forestry technologies to create integrated, diverse, and productive land use systems. The synergy of agroforestry creates enhanced performance, efficiencies, and benefits that cannot be achieved individually in the agricultural or forestry sector. Used extensively in the tropics and with growing use in temperate areas, agroforestry provides many benefits to both landowner and society including crop/livestock/building/road protection, soil and water resource protection, greenhouse gas mitigation, wildlife habitat, recreational opportunities, and alternative income generation, including biofuel production. Serving from its earliest times as a source of fuelwood, agroforestry today offers a variety of options to create diverse, multi-purpose plantings that support energy objectives, as well as other services critical for sustainability of the lands and people. These options range from providing additional conservation services for mitigating adverse impacts from other biofuel production systems to serving as feedstock sources. Short-rotation crops, both woody and herbaceous, are ideally suited for agroforestry. Work in both North America and Europe focuses on the use of agroforestry as a means to create combined energy/food/natural resource systems. Ongoing research at Ontario and Minnesota is exploring the use of new species, species combinations, and performance in different landscape positions as a means to develop more diverse, innovative systems that can provide income generation through the sale of biomass for energy, improved water quality through targeted plantings, and payments for environmental services.

KEY WORDS: alley cropping, conservation, riparian forest buffers, short-rotation crops, windbreaks, working trees

*Corresponding author: University of Guelph, Department of Environmental Biology, Guelph, ON, Canada N1G 2W1; Phone:(519) 824-4120, ext. 52415; Email: agordon@uguelph.ca

SHORT-ROTATION FORESTRY IN GERMANY: LESSONS FROM THE PAST, PRESENT RESEARCH ACTIVITIES, AND FUTURE PERSPECTIVES

Holger Grünewald and Georg von Wühlisch*

Johann Heinrich von Thünen-Institute,
Federal Research Institute for Rural Areas, Forestry and Fishery, Institute of Forest Genetics

Wood has traditionally played a major role in Germany in supplying biomass for energy. Demand for this raw material is expected to rise with new policies promoting renewables. Short-rotation forestry (SRF) is regarded as a promising option to counteract the limited availability of energy wood from traditional forestry. This paper summarizes and reviews Germany's experiences with SRF. Germany lies between 47 °N and 55 °N latitude. In areas generally suitable for SRF, precipitation averages 700 mm but can be as low as 400 mm. The mean temperature there is 9 °C (with a range of 7 to 11°C). Thus, conditions resemble North America in their variability. Enhancing cooperation between Europe and North America is of vital importance for solving common problems. For many sites *Populus* clones are preferable, while *Salix* clones and *Robinia pseudoacacia* increasingly are being used on other sites. Recommendations to match the available clones to available sites need much improvement. For example, satisfactory growth performance has been confirmed for only a few *Populus* clones (e.g., Max, Androscoggin) and under a limited range of conditions. With site-adapted clones, yields of 12 to 16 t dry matter ha^{-1} yr^{-1} can be achieved. Testing and breeding still need to be increased to reach expected production levels. Plantation management and harvesting techniques need to be further developed if SRF is to become an accepted biomass production system. Depending on political support and economic returns SRF is expected to cover an area between 0.5 and 4 million ha of former agricultural land.

KEY WORDS: short-rotation forestry, tree improvement, woody biomass production, *Populus*, *Robinia pseudoacacia*, *Salix*

*Corresponding author: Sieker Landstraße 2, D-22927 Großhansdorf, Germany; Phone: +49 4102 696-106, Fax: +49 4102 696-200, Email: georg.wuehlisch@vti.bund.de

WOODY BIOENERGY SYSTEMS IN THE UNITED STATES

Richard B. Hall

Department of Natural Resource Ecology and Management, Iowa State University

In the United States, dedicated wood biomass cropland is expected to increase to more than 2 million ha with an average production rate of 18 t/ha. Another 334 million dry t/yr can come from forest residues and wood wastes. However, most wood bioenergy crop systems in the United States are still in the early stages of development, with a wide variety of approaches under test in different regions of the country. The most advanced work focused primarily on energy is with willows in New York grown at stand densities of over 14,300 stems/ha with the first commercial harvest at 4 yrs and a total of seven coppice rotations expected. Ten commercial clones are now available and newer clones with up to 40 percent improvement in yield are under test. Work on fast-growing poplar selections and cultural practices for growing them is also well-advanced in several regions of the country with the current emphasis on bioproducts. This production infrastructure will facilitate future shifts to include biofuels. The largest concentration of plantations is in the Pacific Northwest with about 17,000 ha. Cultural practices vary from irrigated plantations, harvested at ages from 6 to 15 yrs for different products, to 11,000 ha planted to primarily one clone (210 clones under test) on 12-yr rotations in Minnesota, to agroforestry plantings of hybrid aspens yielding 22 t/ha in Iowa at 10 yrs of age. A variety of studies show wood biomass energy production to be the most sustainable, environmentally favorable crop that can be grown in many areas, but much research is still needed to answer specific concerns. Major impediments are the time and cost for establishment, competition with annual crops for land, price competition with bioproduct markets, social resistance to monoculture plantations, the need for more efficiency in harvests, and techniques for drying wood for some energy applications.

KEY WORDS: adoption impediments, cultural systems, *Populus, Salix*, yields

*Contact information: Department of Natural Resource Ecology and Management, 339 Science II, Iowa State University, Ames, IA 50011-3221; Phone: (515) 294-1453; Email: rbhall@iastate.edu

*** INVITED SPEAKER ***

THE COUNCIL FOR SUSTAINABLE BIOMASS PRODUCTION

John Heissenbuttel

Interim Director, Council for Sustainable Biomass Production
President, Phoenix Strategic Solutions, Inc.

The Council for Sustainable Biomass Production (CSBP) was initiated in 2007 to ensure that biomass feedstock for cellulosic refineries in the United States is produced in a sustainable manner, balancing economic, environmental, and social imperatives. The CSBP is seeking to generate broad multi-stakeholder consensus on guidelines for sustainability to set this emerging industry on a course of continuous improvement with full support from growers, germplasm providers, social and environmental interests, and refineries. The presentation will provide an overview of CSBP activities to date and its plan for future development and implementation.

KEY WORDS: sustainable, biomass, cellulosic, multi-stakeholder

*Contact information: Phone: (209) 296-4889; Email: hnrc@volcano.net

EFFECT OF LANDSCAPE POSITIONS AND THEIR ASSOCIATED SOIL AND TERRAIN ATTRIBUTES ON BIOMASS CROP YIELD AND GROWTH RATES

Gregg A. Johnson[a,*], Ryan T. Thelemann[a], Haowen Cai[b], Sudipto Banerjee[b], Craig C. Sheaffer[a], Hans-Joachim G. Jung[c], Katie B. Petersen[a], and Ulrike W. Tschirner[d]

[a]Dept. Agronomy and Plant Genetics, University of Minnesota
[b]Biostatistics-Division of SPH, University of Minnesota
[c]USDA Agricultural Research Service, St. Paul, Minnesota
[d]Department of Bioproducts and Biosystems Engineering, University of Minnesota

To advance the use of biomass crops as a feedstock for a wide range of bioindustrial applications, it is essential that we optimize the placement of crops at the field scale in a way that will maximize overall productivity and profitability while addressing critical environmental and ecological issues. The value gained by selective placement of dedicated biomass crops will come from an understanding of how crop growth and productivity are influenced by terrain, soil properties, and other attributes. The ability to predict optimal plant growth across species is critical in developing novel approaches to biomass crop management. We will present information from field research exploring 1) differences in plant growth and development between woody tree species (willow and poplar), a perennial forage legume (alfalfa), a warm-season perennial grass (switchgrass), and a warm-season annual grass (maize) as a function of landscape position; and 2) the relationship between plant growth and environment across seven landscape positions. Results from 2 years of monitoring plant growth and the biomass yield show that landscape position does have an effect on plant growth and development. In addition, our analysis reveals that certain soil and terrain properties affect these yield values differently depending on the crop and/or landscape position. Our use of Bayesian statistical methods in addition to traditional approaches allows us not only to recognize the effects of landscape position properties on biomass crops, but also to predict yield when such landscape position properties are known.

KEY WORDS: landscape position, biomass, Bayesian statistics, willow, poplar, switchgrass

*Corresponding author: University of Minnesota, Southern Research and Outreach Center, 5838 120th Street, Waseca, MN 56093; Phone: (507) 837-5617; Email: johns510@umn.edu

BIOENERGY: AGRICULTURAL CROP RESIDUES

Jane M.F. Johnson

USDA Agricultural Research Service, North Central Soil Conservation Laboratory

The increasing cost of fossil fuels, especially natural gas and petroleum, and a desire to curtail greenhouse gas emissions are driving the expansion of bioenergy. Plant biomass, including woody, grain, and nongrain, are potential energy sources. Prior to the industrial revolution, plant biomass was a major fuel source for heating and cooking. The energy paradigm is shifting to renewable sources of energy, with agronomic and forest products expected to make a significant contribution. The United States is one of the largest producers and users of fuel ethanol, with corn grain the primary feedstock. Critics and proponents alike recognize that alone ethanol from corn grain cannot replace gasoline. Considerable financial and research efforts continue to go into the development of commercially viable cellulosic ethanol production. In addition, utilization of thermochemical platforms (e.g., gasification) is expanding. Regardless of the energy platform, biomass harvest must be conducted in a sustainable manner. The potential risks and benefits vary among the various feed-stocks. Nongrain biomass has other uses, such as animal feed and bedding, protecting the soil from erosive forces, and providing the raw material for maintaining and building soil organic matter. Excess harvest of crop biomass increases the risk of erosion, loss of soil organic matter, and thereby the risk of declining productivity. The amount of biomass inputs required to maintain soil organic carbon exceeds the amount required to limit wind and water erosion to soil tolerance levels. Soil and water conservation benefits must be included in any biomass assessment to prevent long-term environmental damage as the nation seeks near-term solutions to energy problems. Strategies to minimize potential negative impacts of bioenergy while striving to maximize benefits will be discussed.

KEY WORDS: crop residue, bioenergy, soil conservation, renewable energy

*Contact information: Agricultural Research Service, North Central Soil Conservation Laboratory, 803 Iowa Avenue, Morris, MN 56267; Phone: (320) 589-3411; Email: jane.johnson@ars.usda.gov

*** INVITED SPEAKER ***

COMPETITION-INDUCED GROWTH INCREASES IN POPLAR

Jon D. Johnson* and Jeff C. Kallestad

Washington State University-Puyallup

The response of *Populus trichocarpa*, *P. deltoides*, and their interspecific hybrids to competition was studied both in a greenhouse and in the field. The competition response was manipulated by growing trees at close spacing with open-grown trees serving as the control. The competition response is mediated by phytochrome and is a result of decreasing red:far-red ratio as the canopy closes and leaves overlap. Responsive clones showed consistent increases in height, diameter, shoot weight, and specific leaf area. The number of branches and root weight decreased in these same clones. The height growth response was a result of increased internode length; the number of nodes remained unchanged between treatments. In a field study, a measurable response to competition was evident within one week of moving trees from open grown to close spacing. Genetic control of the response was studied in a three-generation pedigree population (Family 331): The *P. trichocarpa* mother was responsive and the *P. deltoides* father was not. In the F_1 parents, one hybrid was responsive and the other not. In the F_2 population, six clones were selected in a stoolbed based on the presence or absence of sylleptic branching. Those without sylleptic branching exhibited statistically longer internodes and were found to be responsive to competition, and those with sylleptic branching were unresponsive in this greenhouse study. If this response could be captured by manipulating field spacing, aboveground productivity could be increased by 20 to 30 percent without any additional cultural inputs.

KEY WORDS: increased productivity, competition, physiological response, phytochrome, red:far-red ratio

*Corresponding author: Washington State University-Puyallup, Department of Natural Resource Sciences, 7612 Pioneer Way East, Puyallup, WA 98371; Email: poplar@wsu.edu

EVALUATING WILLOW AND HYBRID POPLAR CLONES FOR BIOMASS VOLUMES

Allan Jurgens

Saskatchewan Forest Centre

Biomass consumption by various end users in Saskatchewan is on the verge of unprecedented growth. The emerging co-generation, wood pellet, and ethanol industries are exploring both economical and sustainable sources of raw products. Willow and hybrid poplar biomass plantations in other jurisdictions have been shown to produce a substantial amount of wood fiber per acre. In Saskatchewan the use of willows has been limited mainly to shelterbelts. During last several years, interest has increased in the potential use of short-rotation woody crop (SRWC) biomass from willow and hybrid poplar. The Nipawin Biomass Ethanol New Generation Cooperative Ltd. currently has a project in its final stages that is evaluating a catalyst for use in its woody biomass gasification process. Once this catalyst is proven it will substantially increase the demand for using woody biomass to produce ethanol. The Saskatchewan Forest Centre project will evaluate several hybrid willow and hybrid poplar clones at three sites in North Central and North East Saskatchewan. The purpose of this project is to evaluate the volume of each clone produced over several years. All plants will be coppiced after the first year and then a set number will be coppiced every 2 years and every 3 years. Then the volumes will be compared to the other harvesting timelines to determine whether clones harvested annually produce less, more, or the same amount as the harvest timeframe that cuts every 2 years or every 3 years.

KEY WORDS: biomass, willow, hybrid poplar, co-generation, ethanol, biomass volumes, SRWC

*Contact information: Saskatchewan Forest Centre, #101 - 1061 Central Ave., Prince Albert, SK S6V 4V4, Canada; Phone: (306) 765-2852; Email: ajurgens@nrcan.gc.ca or ajurgens@saskforestcentre.ca

ASSESSING HYBRID POPLAR BIOMASS FEEDSTOCK QUALITY USING NEAR INFRARED SPECTROSCOPY AND MULTIVARIATE DATA ANALYSIS

Jeff C. Kallestad and Jon D. Johnson*

Washington State University-Puyallup

Evaluating wood chemical and physical component traits in large-scale breeding programs, and estimating biofeedstock quality for conversion efficiency using standard wet-chemistry techniques is time consuming, cost prohibitive, and impractical. Near infrared spectroscopy (NIRS) together with multivariate statistical analysis has been demonstrated by the pulp and paper industry to rapidly and inexpensively estimate pulp yield, cellulose and lignin content, and wood density to improve manufacturing efficiency. Research by others has demonstrated that NIRS technology can be used to sample live trees nondestructively and spectral analysis of milled increment cores can be used to reliably predict whole-tree wood properties. Utilizing two different portable NIRS systems and multivariate data analysis software we have developed partial least squares calibration equations for cellulose and lignin content in clonal populations of hybrid poplar being developed for cellulosic ethanol conversion. To develop more robust and simplified prediction models, we have used targeted NIR spectral regions for each chemical component, and are investigating the potential of these systems for sampling wood traits *in situ* versus dried and milled increment cores.

KEY WORDS: NIR spectroscopy, predictive model, biofeedstock, cellulosic ethanol

*Corresponding author: Washington State University-Puyallup, Department of Natural Resource Sciences, 7612 Pioneer Way East, Puyallup, WA 98371; Email: poplar@wsu.edu

RYE IN A CELLULOSIC CORN SYSTEM

Michael Kantar* and Paul Porter

University of Minnesota

One of the major concerns with the push toward cellulosic ethanol is the removal of biomass from the system. A potential way to mitigate this loss as well as increase the total amount of biomass produced is to use a fall-planted cereal rye (*Secale cereale* L.) to provide fall ground cover as well as additional biomass in the spring, which can be harvested before planting corn. To investigate the potential of rye to produce biomass three studies were initiated. We first looked at the effect of five different fall planting dates ranging from late August to late October on the biomass accumulation. The dates were chosen to be a range of when growers could plant the rye. Since there has been little effort to breed rye for traits unrelated to grain, the second study investigated rye germplasm for differences in biomass accumulation in different rye cultivars and GRIN (Germplasm Information Network) accessions. Forty-four rye accessions were planted at two planting dates in order to evaluate the germplasm. The third study involves five name cultivars of rye planted on two different dates, representing a recommended planting date and a late planting date, to further evaluate varietal differences in rye. The varieties of winter rye used are Rymin, Homil 21, Vitallo, Spooner, and Aroostock.

KEY WORDS: rye, biomass production, management

*Corresponding author: University of Minnesota, 1991 Upper Buford Circle, St. Paul, MN 55108; Phone: (612) 910-3865; Email: kant0063@umn.edu

CONSERVATION MANAGEMENT STRATEGIES IN ETHANOL CROP PRODUCTION: A BRAZIL-U.S. COMPARISON

Hazen Kazaks

Brown University

Brazil and the United States are the two largest ethanol producers, and in both countries where the majority of ethanol crops are grown are areas of fragmented ecosystems: the Atlantic Forest in Brazil and Prairie Pothole region of the United States. How the farmers use their land and their conservation choices will determine the future state of these natural regions. Additionally, Brazil and the United States will act as a guide to other countries if their ethanol production techniques are reproduced elsewhere. In this study, I interviewed 11 farmers in the state of Paraná and 11 farmers in Iowa on issues of land tenure, labor, and biodiversity, and soil conservation management. Most farmers described their way of life in terms of dollars and cents, but they considered conservation issues as well. At least 7 of 11 Brazilian farms failed to meet a threshold legally mandating 20 percent of farmland be dedicated to its natural state. Almost all Iowa farmers used various USDA retired and working lands conservation programs, and planned on re-enrolling rather than switching to crop production despite currently high commodity prices. However, in 2007, the year of the interviews, nearly all of the corn growers experimented with corn-on-corn rotation on subplots, which removes the nitrogen fixing soybean crop from rotation, and increases inputs. About 25 percent of both Brazilian and American farmers espoused a progressive worldview of farmland management, which included novel soil contouring, no-till techniques, and the need for bottom-up holistic agricultural policy.

KEY WORDS: ethanol production, conservation, farmer decision-making, biodiversity

*Contact information: Brown University, Center for Environmental Studies, Box 1943, 135 Angell Street, Providence, RI 02912 Phone: (530) 220-2518; Email: Hazen_Kazaks@brown.edu

EFFECTS OF A WINTER RYE DOUBLE CROP AFTER CORN SILAGE ON BIOMASS PRODUCTION, WATER QUALITY, AND SOIL NUTRIENT STATUS

Erik Krueger[a,*], Tyson Ochsner[b], Paul Porter[c], Donald Reicosky[d], and John Baker[b]

[a]*Department of Soil, Water, and Climate, University of Minnesota*
[b]*USDA Agricultural Research Service, St. Paul, MN*
[c]*Department of Agronomy and Plant Genetics, University of Minnesota*
[d]*USDA Agricultural Research Service, Morris, MN*

A typical cropping system for confinement dairy production may include consecutive years of corn silage accompanied by annual manure application. Because there is little plant growth for much of the year, this farming system may not achieve maximum annual biomass production. Accompanying high manure application may also lead to soil nutrient buildup, nutrient leaching, and soil erosion. We hypothesize that double-cropping rye after corn silage may maximize annual biomass while addressing the environmental issues associated with corn silage production. Two studies have been designed to test this hypothesis. The first involves cooperation with a large dairy farmer while the other is a small-scale project designed to mimic dairy management practices. On the farm, corn silage production with and without a rye cover crop is compared on adjacent 60-ha fields. The effect of the rye on biomass production, nutrient leaching, and soil nutrient status will be reported. Rye was planted after corn in the fall of 2007 and will be killed prior to corn planting in 2008. At the plot scale, four treatments were compared: corn planted in early May, corn planted in mid-May, corn planted in mid-May after rye, and corn planted in early June after rye. Rye planted October 23 was low yielding in the spring of 2007 and reduced subsequent corn yield. Reduced yield was attributed to lower soil moisture and nitrogen at corn planting. Total biomass from single-cropped corn silage was greater than the double cropped when fall rye growth was limited. Further study is necessary to determine the effectiveness of the double-crop system when rye is established earlier in the fall. The experiment was repeated for 2008 with rye seeded September 14, 2007. If yield can be maximized, this double-cropping system may also have application where corn is grown for energy production.

KEY WORDS: rye, double crop, corn silage, water quality

*Corresponding author: University of Minnesota, Department of Soil, Water, and Climate, 1991 Upper Buford Circle, St. Paul, MN 55108; Phone: (612) 624-8591; Email: krueg226@umn.edu

IMPORTANT DEVELOPMENTS FOR SHORT-ROTATION INTENSIVE CULTURE OF WILLOW IN DIFFERENT REGIONS OF EASTERN CANADA

Michel Labrecque[a,*] and Traian Ion Teodorescu[b]

[a]Institut de recherche en biologie végétale, Montréal Botanical Garden
[b]Institut de recherche en biologie végétale, University of Montréal

The first Canadian willow production systems for bioenergy and bioproducts were established in southern Quebec in the mid-1990s. At that time, research plots of large dimensions (>1 ha) were set up with a plantation design based on a single-row system and a plantation density of 18,000 cutting ha^{-1}. Only one willow clone (*Salix viminalis* 5027) was used in these plantations. Scientific follow-up conducted over several years demonstrates that high biomass yield can be maintained even after multiple, repeated coppicing. Annual yield has been measured at the end of each growing season over the course of this study. Cumulative results over 13 growing seasons show that performances vary according to soil fertility and fertilization level, but overall annual yields between 15 to 22 oven-dried tons (odt) ha^{-1} have been recorded. Differences observed in biomass productivity seem to be largely influenced by climatic conditions. Low rainfall during growing seasons significantly limits willow yields. In each cycle, the biomass yield increment is generally higher between the second and third growing seasons. The encouraging production results from these early experimental trials, as well as the parallel development of diverse environmental applications for willows (sludge treatment, construction of living noise barriers, phytoremediation, etc.) have created enthusiasm and stimulated the deployment of willow biomass crops in many regions of Quebec over the last 5 years. More recently, and with the support of our scientific research group, willow plantations have been established on 11 different sites (total 52 ha) distributed in four climatic zones (from hardiness zone 5 in the south to zone 2 in the Abitibi region) of the province of Quebec. Initial observations of growth parameters reveal excellent performances by *S. miyabeana* (SX64 and SX67) in most of the regions where it has been planted. In some cases, very high yields have been measured (up to 20 odt 2 years following establishment). These results suggest a promising future for the development for SRIC of willows in eastern Canada.

KEY WORDS: willow crops, short rotation intensive culture, *Salix*, growth performances

*Corresponding author: Montréal Botanical Garden, 4101 Sherbrooke East, Montréal, QC, H1X 2B2, Canada; Phone: (514) 872-1862; Email: mlabrecque@jbmontreal.net

ENVIRONMENTAL SERVICES FROM AGROFOREST SYSTEMS: SUSTAINABLE BIOFUEL FEEDSTOCK PRODUCTION IN THE GULF SOUTH REGION OF THE UNITED STATES

Hal O. Liechty[a,*], Michael A. Blazier[b], Philip A. Tappe[a], and Matthew H. Pelkki[a]

[a]University of Arkansas-Monticello
[b]Louisiana State University AgCenter

The Lower Mississippi Alluvial Valley (LMAV) is well suited for large-scale biofuel feedstock production because of its high rainfall, relatively long growing season, central location within the United States, and well developed agricultural infrastructure. Production of common biofuel feedstocks such as corn and soybean require significant inputs of fertilizer, pesticides, and water for irrigation. In addition these crops provide a minimal level of ecosystem services such as carbon sequestration, wildlife habitat, and water quality protection. The LMAV was once dominated by forests, but more than 66 percent of the forest land base has been converted to agriculture production. Conservation efforts have targeted the reforestation of marginal agricultural lands to restore many of the ecosystem services lost through forest conversion. Increased demand for biofuel feedstocks has the potential to limit or reduce the reforestation of these marginal lands. Agroforests could be a flexible and innovative cropping system that could be employed on marginal agricultural land to provide both cellulosic biomass feedstocks and ecosystem services. Agroforest systems composed of varying mixtures of feedstock species, such as cottonwood trees and switchgrass, have the potential to provide a suite of ecological services along with high cellulosic biomass production to meet a variety of management objectives, social constraints, and soil/site conditions. We summarize the potential of agroforest systems to increase biofuel production capacity for the United States, improve economies of economically faltering rural communities of the LMAV, and enhance environmental conditions, such as soil, water, and wildlife habitat quality.

KEY WORDS: biodiversity, nutrient cycling, carbon sequestration, water quality

*Corresponding author: University of Arkansas-Monticello, School of Forest Resources, P.O. Box 3468, Monticello, AR 71656-3468; Phone: (870) 460-1452; Email: liechty@uamont.edu

USING A SYSTEMS APPROACH TO IMPROVE BIOENERGY SUSTAINABILITY ASSESSMENT

Valerie A. Luzadis*, Timothy A. Volk, and Thomas S. Buchholz

College of Environmental Science and Forestry, State University of New York

The current focus on sustainable development and the goal to move from a fossil fuel to a renewable-based economy brings with it the challenge of assessing the sustainability of the wide array of different potential bioenergy systems. Concern about the impact of growing biomass for energy on food security in the poorest regions of the world intensifies the need for reliable, manageable, comprehensive approaches to assessing the sustainability of biomass systems at all scales. Efforts to develop, implement, and revise criteria and indicators to assess the sustainability of forest management provide a foundation for building strong bioenergy sustainability assessment approaches. However, the forest management effort encompasses only one type of feedstock, woody biomass, from one source, naturally occurring forests. It also focuses on only one portion of bioenergy systems, biomass production. While discussion continues, no clear consensus has yet been reached for how to assess bioenergy sustainability. The assessment must focus on all components of the system, from biomass production through useful energy products, and encompass social and economic values. In this paper, we propose a systems approach to more comprehensively inform the development of sustainability criteria and indicators, and to synthesize the many insights from wide-ranging research on biomass-to-energy as well as the associated ranges of social and economic values. Specifically, we present a five-step process for how to use a participatory, systems approach to assess bioenergy sustainability. We suggest that this approach is more comprehensive than the dominant economy-environment-social assessment approach, which is largely ad hoc in nature.

KEY WORDS: sustainability, systems approach, bioenergy

*Corresponding author: State University of New York, Department of Forest and Natural Resources Management, 320 Bray Hall, 1 Forestry Drive, Syracuse, NY 13210; Phone: (315) 470-6693; Email: vluzadis@esf.edu

PRODUCTIVITY AND ENERGY CONTENT OF NATIVE PERENNIAL GRASSLAND SPECIES

Margaret E. Mangan*, Craig C. Sheaffer, Donald L. Wyse, Peter H. Graham,
Ulrike W. Tschirner, and Sanford Weisberg

Department of Agronomy and Plant Genetics, University of Minnesota

Native perennial herbaceous grassland species have been identified as a potential feedstock for energy production. Prairie plants are ideal candidates because they are adapted to low-nutrient environments, generate significant biomass, and provide a plethora of ecological services. Much research has been conducted regarding the productivity of perennial prairie polycultures in natural and restored ecosystems, but there is insufficient information available on the energy conversion potential of individual species. When cellulosic ethanol production is evaluated, it is important to consider the type of polysaccharides in the plant material. The energy industry is interested in the hexose (glucose, galactose, and mannose) and pentose (xylose and arabinose) sugars in biomass feedstocks. At this time ethanol-producing microorganisms cannot convert other monosaccharides (rhamnose, fucose, and uronic acid) to ethanol. In our experiment, we evaluated the distribution of these polysaccharides and the theoretical ethanol yield (according to the National Renewable Energy Laboratory calculator) of multiple native perennial prairie species. Grasses, legumes, and nonleguminous forbs were cultivated alone and in mixtures including one, four, eight, 12, and 24 species. Species were planted into 9-m^2 plots in June 2006 and harvested in fall 2007. We selected *Panicum virgatum, Andropogon gerardii, Sorghastrun nutans, Elymus canadensis, Astragalus canadensis, Helianthus maximilianii,* and *Ratibida pinnata* for chemical composition analysis. Samples were collected from research plots at Lamberton, Waseca, St. Paul, and Becker, MN, and analyzed separately by location. Results from the establishment phase of this experiment show that the energy content of native perennial prairie species varies according to the maturity at harvest and environment. *Panicum virgatum* cultivated at Lamberton, MN, had the greatest overall potential ethanol yield (3,682 L/ha) and *Helianthus maximiliani* at St. Paul had the lowest ethanol yield (52.13 L/ha). The ethanol yields were influenced primarily by biomass yield as well as the distribution of C_5 and C_6 polysaccharides.

KEY WORDS: perennial polycultures, cellulosic ethanol

*Corresponding author: University of Minnesota, Department of Agronomy and Plant Genetics, Room 411 Borlaug Hall, 1991 Upper Buford Circle, St. Paul, MN 55108; Phone: (612) 625-3151; Email: mang0106@umn.edu

PURPOSE-GROWN TREES AS A SUSTAINABLE RENEWABLE ENERGY SOURCE

James Mann

ArborGen, LLC

Bioenergy has been identified as an issue of national importance. Aggressive goals are being set for the use of renewables to displace traditional fuel sources. The 2007 Renewable Fuels Standard mandates the use of 36 billion gallons of renewable fuels by 2022. Today ethanol is produced almost exclusively from corn, but corn is not expected to meet the 36 billion gallon objective. It is projected that 21 billion gallons must come from "advanced biofuels" such as cellulosic ethanol. Cellulosic feedstock must be utilized in order to meet the Renewable Fuels Standard.

Wood, especially from trees grown for industrial forestry, is an excellent source of cellulose and hemicellulose for conversion into ethanol. Purpose-grown trees have several benefits as a biomass feedstock with high growth rates, together with advantages from existing harvest, transport and processing logistics. The high productivity of ArborGen trees allows for the production of more biomass on a smaller land base that can meet supply demands within an area close to the processing facility. Trees provide a "living inventory," eliminating the need for storage and its associated costs while providing a means to smooth supply fluctuations. Additional end uses for trees in the forest products industry provide landowners with flexibility, and leveraging the existing forest products infrastructure provides additional benefits.

ArborGen is developing technologies that will improve productivity, reduce rotation length and total cost, and enhance wood quality of purpose-grown trees. These targets are similar to those that have been defined by the U.S. Department of Energy and others for the long-term feasibility of renewable energy production from cellulosic biomass. ArborGen has trees in development that in the relative near-term are expected to achieve the growth and quality metrics that enable the cost-effective use of woody biomass for the renewable production of biofuel.

KEY WORDS: trees, biotechnology, cellulosic ethanol, pine, *Populus, Eucalyptus*, energy crop

*Contact information: ArborGen, Business and Product Development, P.O. Box 840001, Summerville, SC 29483; Phone: (843) 851-5078; Email: jemann@arborgen.com

*** **INVITED SPEAKER** ***

R&D AND ADOPTION ISSUES FOR FOUR SHORT-ROTATION AFFORESTATION/AGROFORESTRY TECHNOLOGIES: RESULTS OF FOCUS GROUPS CONDUCTED IN QUEBEC AND THE CANADIAN PRAIRIES

Sylvain Masse* and Pierre P. Marchand

Natural Resources Canada - Canadian Forest Service

Through a series of focus groups conducted among landowners of Quebec and the Canadian Prairies, this study identifies perceived R&D and adoption issues for four short-rotation afforestation/ agroforestry technologies for bioenergy generation and other uses. These technologies are: short-rotation intensive culture of willow or hybrid poplar, block plantation of hybrid poplar, willow-based riparian buffer systems, and alley cropping using willow or hybrid poplar. Twenty-three focus groups were conducted with 81 landowners with an early adopter profile. The discussions on each technology were preceded by a popularized presentation on the technology. Besides the notes and recordings of the discussions, a written questionnaire was used to collect specific qualitative information. The exploratory approach designed for the study proved effective and efficient. Perceived advantages and disadvantages were identified. The participants' interest increased for two of the four technologies. The intentions to apply a technology in the short term turned out to be very good for three of the four technologies. The lower intentions expressed for alley cropping reflect the preliminary state of knowledge on this technology. For each of the four technologies, the results allowed us to draw a list of perceived R&D and adoption issues regarding technical, financial, legal, environmental, and other aspects. Since these issues are based on perceptions, their relevance and importance will have to be specified and validated with researchers and other stakeholders. The results also confirmed the importance of specifying the impact of policy frameworks and incentive programs on the adoption of these technologies.

KEY WORDS: short-rotation crops, afforestation, agroforestry, bioenergy, willow, hybrid poplar, social factors

*Corresponding author: Laurentian Forestry Centre, 1055 du P.E.P.S., P.O. Box 10380, Stn. Sainte-Foy, Quebec City, QC, G1V 4C7 Canada; Phone: (418) 648-7152; Email: smasse@nrcan.gc.ca

A MINNESOTA-BASED *POPULUS* BREEDING AND HYBRID POPLAR DEVELOPMENT PROGRAM

Bernard G. McMahon[a,*], William E. Berguson[a], Daniel J. Buchman[a], Thomas E. Levar[a], Craig C. Maly[a], and Timothy C. O'Brien[b]

[a]*University of Minnesota-Duluth, Natural Resources Research Institute*
[b]*University of Minnesota, North Central Research and Outreach Center*

A *Populus* breeding program located at the Natural Resources Research Institute in Duluth, MN, has been producing and testing intra- and inter-specific hybrid poplar germplasm for the past 13 years (1996-2008). The primary *Populus* species of interest for breeding and testing in Minnesota include *P. deltoides, P. nigra, P. maximowiczii,* and *P. trichocarpa.* Eastern cottonwood selections from a previous University of Minnesota collection and from other regional *Populus* improvement programs formed the base breeding population. Genetic diversity of the base population has been increased with open-pollinated seed collections from native trees along Minnesota river-systems and from natural populations located outside the North Central region of the United States. Seed collections and parent materials have been exchanged with cooperators working in northwestern United States, Canada, Europe, and Asia to evaluate long-term parent populations under Minnesota climatic conditions. Potential parent selections are archived in dedicated breeding orchards. Operational logistics of each screening phase from the initial nursery progeny trials through the family field, advanced clonal, and yield block evaluations are explained. Following a 1- to 2-year nursery screening phase, hybrid poplar pedigrees are established in replicated field trials imbedded in commercial fiber farm plantations for critical evaluation throughout the entire rotation period. Growth, disease resistance and ease of establishment are among the selection criteria for new clones for advanced clone and yield testing. Results and trends in terms of growth gains, disease incidence, and clone performance from the current field trials will be presented. Yield gains relative to commercial standards and recommendations for efficient field testing of large populations will be discussed along with opportunities for utilizing new biomass research technologies with the current collections of Minnesota-based germplasm.

KEY WORDS: *Populus* genetics, hybrid poplar, tree breeding, clone development, population improvement

*Corresponding author: 5013 Miller Trunk Highway, Duluth, MN 55811; Phone: (218) 720-2702; Email: bmcmahon@nrri.umn.edu

ECOLOGICAL SERVICES PAYMENTS ENHANCE THE ECONOMIES OF SUSTAINABLY-GROWN FEEDSTOCKS

Linda Meschke

Rural Advantage

A major challenge of sustainable biofuels, bioenergy, and bioproducts production is being able to compete economically with annual crops such as corn, soybeans, or wheat. At this stage, it looks like the amount an energy facility might pay for the biomass feedstock is not enough to drive significant landscape change from annual cropping systems to systems that include perennials. To have successful sustainable agricultural and forest crop bioenergy systems, the production must be able to be economically competitive with the annual crops currently grown. Rural Advantage has developed a concept for how perennial biomass crops can compete with traditional annual crops. This concept provides for a payment to the landowner for a package of ecological services provided by sustainable bioenergy feedstock production to complement the biomass production payment from the energy facility. The concept is a market-based approach for an aggregator to "package" together payments for various ecological services and then make a single payment to the landowner. Ecological services supplied by perennial bioenergy crops for which there currently are markets for include carbon, greenhouse gas emission reductions, nitrogen and phosphorus reductions, habitat improvement, and aquifer recharge/water storage. These market mechanisms exist individually around the globe. Rural Advantage is reviewing these mechanisms and is developing an overall payment package to enable the landowner to get paid for the ecological services provided by perennial bioenergy systems. When payments are packaged together, landowners are able to receive a payment for their ecological services for which they probably would be unable to collect on their own. In addition, the aggregator would be working with presumably several thousand acres and would be able to leverage a higher payment for each service.

KEY WORDS: ecological services, perennial, bioenergy, biomass, feedstocks

*Contact information: 1243 Lake Avenue, Suite 222, Fairmont, MN 56031-1942; Phone: (507) 238-5449; Email: linda@ruraladvantage.org

GROWTH AND YIELD OF POPLAR AND WILLOW HYBRIDS IN THE CENTRAL UPPER PENINSULA OF MICHIGAN

Raymond O. Miller* and Bradford A. Bender

Michigan State University

As demand for woody feedstocks for the production of energy, fuels, and chemicals increases, the need for vigorous and versatile planting stock becomes acute. Because plantations are more expensive to manage than natural forests, yield from planted stands must reliably exceed that of natural stands in order for this production system to be cost competitive. Breeding programs for willow (*Salix* spp.) and poplar (*Populus* var.) have produced taxa that promise superior growth and vitality, but these must be tested more thoroughly in large-plot yield trials and on many more sites before they can be confidently recommended for widespread use. A poplar and a willow yield trial were begun at Michigan State University's Upper Peninsula Tree Improvement Center in Escanaba, MI, in 1998 and 2002, respectively. The results of these trials are summarized here. Five poplar hybrids were included in a large-plot yield study. After 10 years, the best-growing taxa (NM6) had produced an average of 3.7 dry tons per acre-year. Although NM6 grew exceptionally well, it began to develop severe disease problems toward the end of the test. The taxa with the best overall growth and disease resistance (NE222) averaged 2.6 dry tons per acre-year while the standard check taxa (DN34) averaged only 1.7 dry tons per acre-year. In another test, 12 willow taxa were compared in a high-density yield trial. After 6 years, the best-growing taxa (SX61 and SX67) produced 2.5 dry tons per acre-year (averaged over the last 3 years), which was twice the yield of the poorest taxa. These willow yields were comparable to the yield of the healthiest poplar taxa (NE222) mentioned above. NM6 check plots in the willow trial produced 3.4 dry tons per acre-year, which was comparable to the 10-year results for the same taxa summarized above.

KEY WORDS: hybrid poplar, willow, yield, growth, *Populus, Salix*, energy plantation

*Corresponding author: Upper Peninsula Tree Improvement Center, 6005 J Road, Escanaba, MI 49829; Phone: (906) 786-1575; Email: rmiller@msu.edu

RESPONSE OF THREE *SALIX* VARIETIES TO IRRIGATION WITH DIFFERENT CONCENTRATIONS OF SOLVAY STORM WATER

Jaconette Mirck* and Timothy A. Volk

College of Environmental Science and Forestry, State University of New York

The production of soda ash, using the Solvay process, resulted in the creation of 600 ha of wastebeds near Syracuse, NY, over a 100-year period. Chloride leaching from the Solvay wastebeds into surrounding water bodies, including Onondaga Lake, is a concern. Storm water/snowmelt needs to be recycled onto an evapotranspiration (ET) cover on the wastebeds during the summer. To assess this, a greenhouse experiment was carried out. The experiment was a 6×3 factorial design with four replications. The first factor consisted of six treatments, five concentrations of Solvay storm water based on chloride concentrations ($8{,}000$ mg Cl^- L^{-1} to 160 mg Cl^- L^{-1}) and a control of tap water, and the second of the three varieties of shrub willow. The objectives were to 1) measure physical and physiological plant characteristics to determine which are stress indicators and to quantify the response of willow to storm water using these indicators; 2) assess the impact of storm water concentration on evapotranspiration and the difference between willow varieties; and 3) quantify the effects of willow variety on the uptake of calcium, magnesium, sodium, and chloride. Biomass accumulation, stomatal conductance (after 4.5 weeks), and evapotranspiration decreased for the treatments with the highest storm water concentration. Sodium concentrations for the highest treatment were 3 to 8 times higher for the leaves and 6 to 9 times for the shoots compared to the control, and chloride concentrations were 14 to 32 times for the leaves and 2 to 6 times for the shoots compared to the control. All willow varieties survived the 10-week experiment, but the willows that received the highest treatment showed signs of stress after 8 weeks. This experiment will assist in the design of an ET cover on the Solvay wastebeds and the potential for recycling storm water through shrub willows.

KEY WORDS: *Salix*, phytoremediation, Solvay wastebeds, salts

*Corresponding author: State University of New York, College of Environmental Science and Forestry, Department of Forest and Natural Resources Management, 244 Illick Hall, SUNY-ESF, 1 Forestry Drive, Syracuse, NY 13210; Phone: (315) 470-6757/6775; Email: jmirck@syr.edu

BIOMASS PRODUCTION FROM NATIVE WARM-SEASON GRASS MONOCULTURES AND POLYCULTURES MANAGED FOR BIOENERGY

Rob Mitchell* and Kenneth Vogel

USDA Agricultural Research Service, Grain, Forage, and Bioenergy Research Unit

Switchgrass monocultures grown for bioenergy lack plant species diversity and may not optimize ecosystem services. However, switchgrass monocultures are generally perceived to be more productive and provide fewer establishment and management challenges than polycultures. Our objective was to compare the dry matter production and persistence of monocultures and polycultures of native warm-season grasses managed for bioenergy in the Great Plains. This study was conducted in 2004, 2005, 2006, and 2007 at Mead and Clay Center, NE. Five native warm-season grasses (big bluestem, indiangrass, switchgrass, little bluestem, and sideoats grama) were seeded in monocultures and polycultures. Monocultures of each species were compared with polycultures consisting of each species at 20-percent increments in the seeding mixture. Sixty-eight mixtures were seeded in 2004 and 2005 in four replicates at each location for a total of 1,088 plots. Species composition for each plot was determined in autumn 2007. Dry matter production was determined at peak production during the seeding year and for 2 or 3 years after seeding, depending on planting year. Stand persistence was measured in spring 2008. Biomass production patterns will provide guidance regarding what native warm-season grasses should be grown to optimize long-term production and potentially increase plant species diversity in stands managed for bioenergy.

KEY WORDS: herbaceous perennials, switchgrass, genetics, feedstocks

*Corresponding author: University of Nebraska-Lincoln, 362F Plant Science, Lincoln, NE 68583; Phone: (402) 472-1546; Email: rob.mitchell@ars.usda.gov

HERBACEOUS BIOMASS: STATE OF THE ART

Kenneth J. Moore

Department of Agronomy, Iowa State University

Meeting the U.S. Departments of Agriculture and Energy's goal of replacing 30 percent of transportation energy by 2030 with cellulosic biofuels will require development of highly productive energy crops. It is estimated that a billion-ton annual supply of biomass of all sources will be required to meet this goal, which represents a fivefold increase over currently available biomass. Under one scenario, dedicated energy crops yielding an average of 8 dry tons/yr are projected to be planted on 55 million acres. Switchgrass (*Panicum virgatum* L.) is a perennial native grass that has received substantial interest as a potential energy crop due to its wide adaptation. However, it produces relatively low yields on productive soils and has other limitations related to seed dormancy and establishment. More recently, Miscanthus (*Miscanthus × giganteus*) has been touted as a potential energy crop. A warm-season perennial grass native to Southeastern Asia, it has relatively high yield potential when grown on productive soils. However, it is a sterile hybrid that must be propagated vegetatively and requires a few years to achieve maximum production. Both species have potential as dedicated energy crops, but require further improvement and development. Other crops with high potential for cellulosic energy are photoperiod-sensitive sorghum (*Sorghum bicolor* (L.) Moench) and corn (*Zea mays* L.) cultivars. Vegetative development of these cultivars occurs over a longer period in temperate regions and they produce little or no viable seed. A rational long-term approach will be required to develop alternative, high-yielding biomass crops specifically designed for energy and industrial uses. A significant research effort is needed to identify alternative plant species that produce higher biomass yields and have desirable biomass traits, develop cultivated varieties of alternative species through genomics and plant breeding approaches, and develop appropriate crop management practices and systems for producing dedicated energy crops.

KEY WORDS: biomass, bioenergy, switchgrass, *Miscanthus*, sorghum, corn

*Contact information: Iowa State University, Department of Agronomy, 1571 Agronomy Hall, Ames, IA 50011; Phone: (515) 294-5482; Email: kjmoore@iastate.edu

*** INVITED SPEAKER ***

USE OF SELECTED HYBRID POPLARS IN SHORT-ROTATION WOODY CROPS PRODUCTION: THE EUROPEAN EXPERIENCE FROM THE FIELD TO THE FINAL TRANSFORMER

Fabrizio Nardin* and Franco Alasia

Alasia Franco Vivai, Savigliano (CN), Italy

Producing green energy through the use of woody biomass from short-rotation forestry gives farmers an interesting alternative to traditional crops while reducing reliance on fossil fuels. In Italy, the cultivation of hybrid poplar for woody biomass in short-rotation coppice (2 to 5 years) is a business opportunity for farmers and technicians involved in the production cycle, from the field to the power plant.

The *Populus* genus is well suited for short-rotation forestry, especially because of the potential for increased yields and disease tolerance through genetic improvement systems. For more than 20 years, this topic has been at the center of activity at Alasia Franco Vivai, an Italian company from northwestern Italy. High-performance plant material has made the production of woody biomass increasingly more attractive to farmers. New equipment has been developed for planting, cultivating, and harvesting operations, and species-specific agricultural techniques have been applied. The combined use of very productive poplar clones and appropriate agricultural practices gives high yields. Italy, with an area of more than 6,000 hectares, is the European country with the most land for short-rotation poplar coppices and the model that has been developed there will be exported to other countries around the world.

KEY WORDS: genetic improvement, hybrid poplar, yield, mechanization, chipwood

*Corresponding author: Alasia Franco Vivai, strada Solerette 5/A, 12038 Savigliano (CN) - Italy; Phone +39 3356907316; Email: info@alasifranco.it

PROLONGED PLANTING SEASON IN WILLOW SHORT-ROTATION FORESTRY: EFFECTS ON INITIAL PLANT GROWTH AND PLANT SURVIVAL

Nils-Erik Nordh*, Pär Aronsson, and Theo Verwijst

Swedish University of Agricultural Sciences

The recommended time for planting willow (*Salix* sp) in Swedish short-rotation forestry (SRF) is from early spring (April) to early summer (mid-June). After early planting, willow cuttings may take advantage of the high soil-moisture content and the longer establishment season. However, early planting increases the risk of frost damage during cold nights that may occur during this time. The start of the planting season varies between years depending on when the soil becomes dry enough to be harrowed and reached by the planting machine. Thereafter the planting may be delayed due to rainy periods or drought. In the worst case the planting may have to be postponed until next year. A longer planting season would justify the establishment of SRF and planting machines could be used more efficiently. This study, performed on three willow clones during 2007-2008 at two locations in Sweden, investigates the effects of a prolonged planting season on initial plant growth and survival. Planting was done 11 times every third week from May 2 to November 20. Individual plant development was assessed every week and survival, sprouting, number of shoots, and damage were recorded. First-year plant growth was measured nondestructively after growth cessation and second-year plant growth will be measured in winter 2008. The initial results show that plant survival in general decreases rapidly when planting after mid-July and that first year biomass production gradually declines after the first planting date. Therefore, our preliminary conclusion is that early planting should be recommended.

KEY WORDS: biomass, establishment, planting time, *Salix*, shoot sprouting

*Corresponding author: Swedish University of Agricultural Sciences, Department of Crop Production Ecology, Box 7043, S-75007 Uppsala, Sweden; Phone: +46 (18) 672561; Email: Nils-Erik.Nordh@vpe.slu.se

STRATEGIC ASSESSMENT OF BIOFUELS POTENTIAL FOR THE WESTERN U.S.

Marcia Patton-Mallory[a,*], Richard Nelson[b], Ken Skog[a], Bryan Jenkins[c], Nathan Parker[c], Peter Tittmann[c], Quinn Hart[c], Ed Gray[d], Anneliese Schmidt[d], and Gayle Gordon[e]

[a]*U.S. Forest Service*
[b]*Kansas State University*
[c]*University of California, Davis*
[d]*Antares*
[e]*Western Governor's Association*

The technical feasibility of producing biofuels in the western United States is described using spatially explicit biomass resource supply curves, a detailed transportation network model for the region, and costs for converting biomass to refined biofuels. The study addresses the widespread concern over the environmental, geopolitical, and economic effects of the U.S. dependence on petroleum. The study is responding to state and federal legislative bodies who are setting goals for reducing the consumption of fossil fuels in the transportation sector using targets for the infusion of so-called "low-carbon" biofuels into the transportation fuel market. The use of biomass from municipal waste streams, forest thinnings, and herbaceous agricultural residues or energy crops for biofuels production can significantly reduce the net life cycle emissions of greenhouse gases in comparison with crude oil; the benefits from grain and other crops are less certain. This report and the accompanying models represent a significant step forward in understanding the potential for meeting policy goals based on near-term technological and infrastructure parameters. The paper presents biofuel supply curves estimating potential future supplies of liquid fuels from biomass in the western United States as a function of market price. The combined GIS network analysis and biorefinery optimization model was developed to:

- Spatially resolve biomass resource quantities and distributions throughout the Western Governor's Association region for major feedstock types,

- Map supporting transportation and biofuel-handling infrastructure to estimate biorefinery gate feedstock costs and biofuel distribution costs,

- Optimize biorefinery types, sizes, and locations for competing conversion technologies based on the objective of maximizing producer profit under a market price constraint.

The analysis focuses on the generation of biomass and biofuel supply curves over a year 2015 planning horizon. Total capacity for biofuels production is described for both the regional and state levels.

KEY WORDS: biofuels, agriculture residues, wood residues, thinnings, grease, herbaceous energy crops, biomass supply estimates, network analysis

*Corresponding author: U.S. Forest Service, Biomass and Bioenergy Coordinator, 2150 Centre Ave, Building A, Fort Collins, CO 80526; Phone: (970) 295-5947; Email: mpattonmallory@fs.fed.us

IMPACT OF GROWTH ENVIRONMENT VARIABILITY ON ALFALFA YIELD, CELLULOSIC ETHANOL TRAITS, AND PAPER PULP CHARACTERISTICS

Katie B. Petersen[a,*], Ryan T. Thelemann[a], Hans-Joachim G. Jung[a,b], Ulrike W. Tschirner[a], Craig C. Sheaffer[a], and Gregg A. Johnson[a]

[a]University of Minnesota
[b]USDA Agricultural Research Service, St. Paul, MN

Alfalfa is a promising bioenergy feedstock due to its high yield, nitrogen-fixation capacity, high net energy ratio, potential for planting in rotation with corn, and valuable protein co-product (leaf meal). Our objective was to examine the effect of growth environment on biomass yield, cellulosic ethanol traits, and paper pulp fiber characteristics of alfalfa. Landscape position (hilltop and mild slope), season of harvest (four harvests/year), and multiple years (2005 and 2006) were sources of environmental variation with two replicates of each landscape position. Alfalfa was harvested at bud maturity stage to determine whole herbage yield and stem proportion. Alfalfa stem samples were analyzed for cell-wall carbohydrate and lignin concentration. A lab-scale conversion test was developed to assess differences in susceptibility to sugar release for ethanol production via dilute acid/high-temperature pretreatment and enzymatic saccharification. Stems were also de-fibered using Franklin Solution to measure relevant fiber characteristics (fiber length, width, and fines). Yield varied across harvests in 2005 (880 to 3,840 kg ha^{-1}) and 2006 (2,400 to 9,520 kg ha^{-1}) with higher yields in 2006. Stem proportion was less variable between years, but typically declined with later harvests (23 to 54.8 percent). Cell-wall glucose concentration varied dramatically across harvests and years (197.8 to 321.9 g kg^{-1} DM) and glucose release efficiency was similarly variable (45.1 to 84.7 percent). Xylose concentration (60 to 112.5 g kg^{-1} DM) and release (59.8 to 82.2 percent) were also variable among harvests and years. Pulp fiber length did not vary with growth environment; however, fiber width and fines content differed among harvests and years. Landscape position was not a significant source of variation for alfalfa biomass trait. Industries hoping to utilize alfalfa biomass, harvested multiple times each year, for cellulosic ethanol and paper manufacturing must be prepared for significant feedstock quality variation due to growth environment.

KEY WORDS: alfalfa, environment, yield, cellulosic ethanol, fiber length

*Corresponding author: University of Minnesota, Department of Agronomy and Plant Genetics, 411 Borlaug Hall, 1991 Upper Buford Circle, St. Paul, MN 55108; Phone: (612) 625-7776; Email: pete5953@tc.umn.edu

CHARACTERIZATION OF ARSENIC UPTAKE UNDER PHOSPHORUS SUFFICIENT AND DEFICIENT CONDITIONS IN SHRUB WILLOW (*SALIX* SPP.) CLONES OF DIFFERING AS SENSITIVITIES

Emily E. Pulley and Lawrence B. Smart*

State University of New York, College of Environmental Science and Forestry

Hydroponic studies of phosphorus (P) and arsenic (As) uptake by plants consistently demonstrate that the presence of P results in less As uptake. Transport of the structurally analogous ionic forms of these elements occurs via phosphate transporters, which are encoded by a multigene family. A second consensus result is that As nontolerant species or populations accumulate more As at a faster rate than As-tolerant counterparts. We hypothesized that a P-deficient (-P) pretreatment would increase phosphate transporter activity, thus increasing As uptake when introduced in hydroponic culture. We also hypothesized that an As nontolerant willow clone would have higher tissue As concentrations than a tolerant clone. A 2×2×2×2 factorial experiment was designed to investigate As uptake in shrub willow (*Salix* spp.) clones of varying As tolerances in relation to P status. When As was added without P, the As nontolerant clone, 00X-026-082 (*S. eriocephala*), wilted within 1 day of As exposure, while the tolerant clone, 99202-011 (*S. viminalis* × *S. miyabeana*), took 6 days to wilt, reinforcing previously established relative tolerances. Clonal differences may also represent differing intracellular P concentrations to maintain homeostasis. In contrast to results from other species, the presence of P increased As concentration and content in both willow clones. This result may have been related to slower As uptake or increased plant nutrition and biomass in +P treatments. The duration of As exposure complicates interactions between factors, as the time scale of the treatment was longer than the time scale of initial membrane transport kinetics.

KEY WORDS: biomass, hydroponics, phosphate, phytoremediation

*Corresponding author: State University of New York, College of Environmental Science and Forestry, Department of Environmental and Forest Biology, 246 Illick Hall, Syracuse, NY 13210;
Phone: (315) 470-6737; Fax: (315) 470-6934; Email: lbsmart@esf.edu

IMPACTS OF PAPER SLUDGE, MANURE, AND FERTILIZER APPLICATION ON SOIL PROPERTIES AND BIOMASS PRODUCTION IN A SHORT ROTATION WILLOW CROPPING SYSTEM IN CENTRAL NEW YORK

Amos K. Quaye[a,*], Timothy A. Volk[a], Sasha D. Hafner[b], Don J Leopold[a], and Charles D. Schirmer[a]

[a]College of Environmental Science and Forestry, State University of New York
[b]HydroQual, Inc.

Land application of organic wastes to short-rotation woody crops (SRWC) can reduce the environmental impacts associated with waste disposal and enhance biomass production. A complete understanding of the potential impacts of organic amendments, however, requires the examination of changes in soil characteristics and plant productivity to these amendments. This study was conducted to evaluate the response of shrub willow (*Salix × dasyclados*; SV1) to organic amendments in central New York, and to determine the impacts of the amendments on soil chemical properties. Treatments were applied in the spring of 2005 to two fields of SV1 at different growth stages. The older field was 1 year above ground on a 10-year-old root system, and the younger field was a regrowth after first coppice. The treatments were: 100 kg N/ha as urea (I), 100 kg total N/ha as dairy manure (ML), 100 kg available N/ha as dairy manure (MH), 100 kg total N/ha as paper sludge (S), 100 kg total N/ha sludge + 100 kg available N/ha of manure (SM) and Control (C). Generally there was no productivity gain due to organic amendment, nor did nitrogen-poor sludge depress yields. There was significant treatment effect on foliar Ca ($P = 0.03$) and S ($P = 0.03$) in the older field and significant ($P = 0.018$) negative effect on foliar P in the younger field. Other foliar elements were affected by fertilization. There was significant treatment effect on soil Ca, Mg, and pH ($P < 0.0001$, 0.007, 0.002, respectively) and marginally significant effect for organic matter ($P = 0.07$) in the older field. Soil Ca and pH were significantly ($P = 0.05$, 0.02, respectively) affected by fertilization in the younger field. The low response to N fertilization could partly be explained by the relatively high internal nutrient recycling of the fields and low levels of rainfall during the summer of the application year.

KEY WORDS: shrub willow, waste management, biomass production, *Salix*, organic amendment

*Corresponding author: State University of New York, College of Environmental Science and Forestry, Department of Forest and Natural Resources Management, 1 Forestry Dr., Syracuse NY, 13210; Phone: (315) 470-6775; Email: akquaye@syr.edu

HIGH THROUGHPUT ANALYSIS METHODS FOR SHORT-ROTATION CROPS

Timothy G. Rials* and Nicole Labbé

The Institute of Agriculture, University of Tennessee

While biomass yield is a convenient measure of the potential of short-rotation crops as feedstock for bioenergy and biofuels, other characteristics may ultimately determine overall quality for a particular conversion platform. Chemical composition, especially total sugars, will impact ethanol yield from biochemical processes. Inorganic compounds present in the biomass will influence the amount and type of residue from thermochemical conversion methods like pyrolysis and gasification. Information on these fundamental measures of biomass quality is limited, largely because of the time and expense associated with the laboratory techniques required to determine the chemical, physical, and mechanical properties of lignocellulosic material. Recently, several spectroscopy techniques have been developed as high-throughput analytical tools that make it possible to quickly determine fundamental characteristics of biomass, including chemical composition.

Near Infrared Spectroscopy (NIRS) and Laser-Induced Breakdown Spectroscopy (LIBS) are of particular utility because of the complementary information they provide, and because they are both rugged and robust instruments. NIRS provides data on the organic matrix, and LIBS on the inorganic composition of biomass. Recent advances in the use of multivariate statistical methods for analysis make it possible to obtain the complete chemistry of the biomass. Projection to latent structures modeling allows development of calibration curves to predict the properties of interest. Typical correlation coefficients (R^2) for cellulose content predicted from NIRS data are 0.90 or above. Importantly, this capability reduces the time for analysis to seconds, and the expense to pennies. This presentation will describe applications of high-throughput methods for biomass assessment, and discuss the implications for future advances.

KEY WORDS: chemical composition, spectroscopy techniques, multivariate analysis

*Corresponding author: University of Tennessee, Institute of Agriculture, Forest Product Center and Sun Grant Center, 2506 Jacob Drive, Knoxville, TN 37996-4570; Phone: (865) 946-1130; Email: trials@utk.edu

SUGAR/ENERGY CANES AS FEEDSTOCKS FOR THE BIOFUELS INDUSTRY

Ed Richard, Jr.*, Thomas Tew, Robert Cobill, and Anna Hale

USDA Agricultural Research Service, Southern Regional Research Center, Sugarcane Research Lab

It is widely acknowledged that technologies for the conversion of the ligno-cellulosic component of the plant will have to be developed if the United States is to replace some of its needs for transportation fuel with renewable sources of biofuels. Sugar cane is cultured as a perennial row crop in the southern areas of Florida, Louisiana, and Texas. Since 1795, it has been grown, harvested, and processed for commercial sugar recovery in Louisiana, which lies farther from the equator than almost any area where this tropical crop is grown. Sugar cane is a very efficient C_4 grass in converting sunlight and other inputs into biomass—biomass that includes a high percentage of sugar that can be easily converted to ethanol as demonstrated by the successes in Brazil. Three sugar cane varieties (L 79-1002, HoCP 91-552, and Ho 00-961), dropped from the sugar cane varietal development program because of excessive fiber levels, were released in 2007 as "bench-marking energy cane varieties" to meet the possible needs of biorefineries, where the production of ethanol from all of the aboveground components of the crop is the desired objective. The three varieties produced soluble sugar yields of 10.5 to 14.8 t/ha and dry fiber (bagasse) yields of 13.0 to 20.8 t/ha with an estimated total ethanol yield of 11,400 to 13,400 L/ha when averaged over four yearly fall harvests of the same planting. New varieties of dedicated energy canes with higher levels of cold tolerance and higher fiber yields are being developed by introgressing genes from sugar cane's wild relative, *Saccharum spontaneum*, and from its near relatives *Miscanthus* and *Erianthus* in an attempt to move the geographic range of adaption further northward. Some of these early-generation hybrids are being tested in Alabama, Arkansas, California, Mississippi, and Oklahoma, as well as more northern areas of the traditional cane-growing states. Other types of sugar-containing grasses are also being evaluated as complementary crops to lengthen the season for feedstock deliveries and reduce storage costs at the biorefinery. Among these are four sweet sorghum varieties (Dale, M 81-E, Theis, and Topper) and two essentially nonflowering sorghum × sudangrass forage hybrids (MMR 333/27 and MMR 333/47). When these sorghums were planted in the early spring and harvested in the mid to late summer prior to sugar cane harvest (approximately 140 days after planting), soluble sugar and dry biomass yields of 8.1 and 15.7 Mg/ha were obtained with estimated total (sugar plus fiber) ethanol yields averaging 11,300 and 11,200 L/ha for the sweet and forage sorghums, respectively. Of the total ethanol produced, 50 percent of the sweet sorghum's ethanol yield was derived from sugar while for the forage sorghums only 34 percent was produced from sugar.

KEY WORDS: sugarcane, sweet sorghum, sorghum × sudangrass forage hybrids, *Miscanthus, Erianthus*, ethanol production

*Corresponding author: 5883 USDA Road, Houma, LA 70360; Phone: (985) 872-5042; Email: ed.richard@ars.usda.gov

*** INVITED SPEAKER ***

PRODUCTION OF BIOMASS FOR ENERGY FROM SUSTAINABLE FORESTRY SYSTEMS: CANADA AND EUROPE

Jim Richardson

IEA Bioenergy Task 31 and Poplar Council of Canada

Forest ecosystems are the world's largest accessible source of biomass. Under varying levels of management intensity, much of this biomass is used for conventional forest products such as lumber, pulp, and panels. Throughout most of the developing world, forest biomass is also harvested for energy, and for cooking, heat, and other daily needs. Increasingly in the western industrialized world also, interest is focused on the forest as a feedstock for bioenergy, a sustainable, carbon-neutral alternative to fossil energy. Forest biomass for energy may come from harvesting residues, from silvicultural treatments or from utilization of otherwise unmerchantable species or assortments. To be truly sustainable, forest systems harvesting biomass for energy must consider nutrient cycling, wood ash recycling, carbon sequestration, stand productivity, and soil and water conservation, as well as cost-efficient forest operations. Social and cultural issues must also be taken into account. In many jurisdictions, policy and tax measures can help to make this form of renewable energy a viable alternative. Using biomass for energy from existing forestry systems is an alternative to growing short-rotation woody crops specifically for energy purposes. It is particularly suited to regions such as northern Europe and Canada, where forest resources are abundant. Natural phenomena which may be associated with climate change may provide significantly enhanced availability of such forest biomass, but sustainability of supply must always be considered.

KEY WORDS: forestry systems, forest biomass, sustainability, environment, socio-economics

*Contact information: 1876 Saunderson Dr., Ottawa, ON, K1G 2C5, Canada; Phone: (613) 521-1995; Email: jrichardson@on.aibn.com

*** INVITED SPEAKER ***

PACIFIC NORTHWEST POPLARS:
A RESILIENT ARTHROPOD COMMUNITY AND THE DISTRIBUTION OF INSECT-CAUSED MORTALITY IN CUTTINGS

R. Andrew Rodstrom*, John J. Brown, and John R. Rodstrom

Department of Entomology, Washington State University

Hybrid poplars are a long-rotation (12-15 yr) woody crop grown to meet today's fiber demands. To meet the recent push toward environmentally friendly management, several poplar plantations in the Pacific Northwest have been certified by the Forest Stewardship Council (FSC), which encourages environmentally responsible management of forest resources. A two-part project was conducted to investigate how terrestrial arthropod communities in FSC-certified poplar plantations respond to the planned catastrophe of harvest and how cutting mortalities were distributed within a planting unit. Terrestrial arthropod communities were surveyed using unbaited pitfall traps in pre- and post-harvest habitats. A Shannon-Weiner diversity index was used to evaluate community composition of the pre- and post-harvest community. Cuttings were surveyed on foot, with failed cuttings being marked by a surveyor's flag and recorded on a map of the planting unit. Using Spatial Analysis and Decision Assistance (SADA) we discerned patterns of insect-caused cutting failure within individual units.

Results show that arthropod communities recover to preharvest levels in less than 2 years, indicating resilience to the disturbance. Despite the environmental catastrophe of harvest, the most common species in the system was found across all communities. The monospecific dominance of *Calathus ruficollis* (Coleoptera: Carabidae) was most noticeable in the fall, with spring and summer communities showing greater evenness. We found that patterns of cutting failure were consistent for a given pest across all units. These findings suggest that insect-caused cutting failures occur in discernable patterns linked to specific pests. Our illustration of insect-caused cutting failure through SADA allows the growers to identify problem areas within the farms and address pest problems within individual units based on failure patterns.

KEY WORDS: hybrid poplar, community resilience, pest distribution, *Calathus ruficollis*

*Corresponding author: Washington State University, Department of Entomology, 166 FSHN, Pullman, WA 99164; Phone: (509) 335-2129; Email: andrewrodstrom1@yahoo.com

IMPACTS OF BIOFUEL PRODUCTION ON GRASSLAND BIRDS IN WISCONSIN

David W. Sample[a],* and Christine A. Ribic[b]

[a]Wisconsin Department of Natural Resources
[b]U.S. Geologic Survey, Wisconsin Cooperative Wildlife Research Unit

As interest in producing ethanol from corn as a way to achieve energy independence rises in the Midwest, there is growing concern among ecologists in Wisconsin and surrounding states that we should be cautious in our approach to the development of biofuels. Impacts on natural resources are important factors to consider in the debates over what and where different types of biofuel production should be developed. In Wisconsin, grassland conservation is important due to both the value of grasslands for a variety of native flora and fauna and the threats to these vulnerable habitats. Some of the areas with the best opportunities for managing grasslands in Wisconsin have the potential to be negatively impacted by large-scale biofuel production. This situation is the result of multiple factors: an increase in the amount of corn acres, the potential for establishment of tree plantations in former prairie landscapes, the accelerated loss of pasture habitats, and a decrease in grassland acres enrolled in the USDA Conservation Reserve Program. Grassland birds are an important conservation target due to their wide-scale population declines. Our work in Wisconsin shows that landscape composition plays a role in patterns of grassland bird occupancy. Specifically, we know that grassland bird densities decrease in landscapes dominated by row crop agriculture or high amounts of woods. Growing switchgrass or mixes of native prairie grasses and forbs for biofuels as an alternative to corn has potential for reducing impacts on natural resources in open agricultural landscapes. However, more research is needed to understand the implications of biofuel production on grassland conservation at a landscape scale.

KEY WORDS: grassland birds, biofuel, switchgrass, conservation, landscape

*Corresponding author: Wisconsin Department of Natural Resources, 2801 Progress Road, Madison, WI 53716; Phone: (608) 221-6351; Email: david.sample@wisconsin.gov

*** INVITED SPEAKER ***

CHALLENGES ASSOCIATED WITH SHORT-ROTATION BIOFUEL PLANTATION ESTABLISHMENT IN THE LOWER MISSISSIPPI ALLUVIAL VALLEY

Jamie L. Schuler*, Matthew H. Pelkki, and H. Christoph Stuhlinger

University of Arkansas-Monticello

The development of biofuel synthesis technologies has led to increased interest in woody crops grown specifically for energy production. These woody feedstocks typically involve fast-growing species (e.g., *Salix* spp., *Populus* spp.) planted at high densities using short rotations and intensive cultural practices like weed control and fertilization. Under ideal conditions, this type of system can produce 10+ dry tons/ac/yr, which is substantially higher than the 2.5 to 4 dry tons/ac/yr produced by pine plantations in the southern United States. Many of these plantings are projected to be established on lower quality agricultural lands. Recent attempts at establishing these plantations have highlighted some of the challenges (and expectations) that landowners will need to overcome in order to achieve levels of production that are financially attractive. This paper will address some of the pitfalls and hurdles that need to be overcome before woody biofuel plantations will become widespread.

KEY WORDS: short-rotation woody crops, SRWC, bioenergy plantations, plantation establishment

*Corresponding author: University of Arkansas-Monticello, School of Forest Resources, P.O. Box 3468, Monticello, AR 71656; Phone: (870) 460-1448; Email: schuler@uamont.edu

A NATIONAL ASSESSMENT OF CURRENT AND FUTURE STATE OF TECHNOLOGY FOR WOODY CROPS IN MEETING MANDATED BIOFUEL REQUIREMENTS

Anna M. Shamey, Robert D. Perlack*, and Lynn L. Wright

Oak Ridge National Laboratory

Efforts are under way to assess the potential contribution of woody crops in meeting mandated cellulosic and advanced biofuel requirements of the recently passed Energy Independence and Security Act of 2007 (EISA). EISA requires the use of 21 billion gallons of cellulosic and other advanced biofuels by 2022. The cellulosic feedstocks required to produce these biofuels can come from a wide variety of cropland and forest land sources and because EISA specifies use rather than production, imports can also be used to satisfy the mandate. The impact of EISA on U.S. agriculture and forestry will very much depend on the relative proportions of cropland- and forest land-derived feedstock and the extent to which imports are used to meet the mandate. This paper examines the potential contribution of short-rotation woody crops in meeting the EISA mandate. The paper provides an assessment of the current state of the technology for producing woody crops, realistic scenarios of technological change that may impact production technology in 2022, and results of a spatial analysis that show areas of the country where woody crops are most likely to be economically competitive. Included in these results are likely changes in land use (e.g., what land uses are most likely to be displaced) and associated impacts on sustainability and greenhouse gas emissions. The paper is national in scope and thus relies on geographic information system techniques to summarize results.

KEY WORDS: woody crops, short-rotation, economics, productivity, spatial analysis, land use change

*Corresponding author: Oak Ridge National Laboratory, Environmental Sciences Division, P.O. Box 2008, Building 1062, Oak Ridge, TN 37831-6422; Phone: (865) 574-5186; Email: perlackrd@ornl.gov

WOOD-TO-WHEELS: A MULTIDISCIPLINARY RESEARCH INITIATIVE IN SUSTAINABLE TRANSPORTATION UTILIZING FUELS AND CO-PRODUCTS FROM FOREST RESOURCES

David R. Shonnard[a],*, Jeffrey D. Naber[b], Qiong Zhang[c], Ann L. Maclean[d], Kathleen E. Halvorsen[e], and John W. Sutherland[b]

[a]*Department of Chemical Engineering, Michigan Technological University (MTU)*
[b]*Department of Mechanical Engineering-Engineering Mechanics, MTU*
[c]*Sustainable Futures Institute, MTU*
[d]*School of Forest Resources and Environmental Science, MTU*
[e]*Department of Social Sciences, MTU*

Michigan Technological University (MTU) has established a broad-based university-wide research initiative, termed Wood-to-Wheels (W2W), to develop improved technologies for growing, harvesting, converting, and using woody biomass in renewable transportation fuel applications. MTU has established advanced facilities for biomass production and processing and biofuels-focused powertrain testing in support of the W2W research initiative. Research related to biotechnology, forest ecosystem management, vehicular systems, and decision-making sustainability include:

- Sustainable forest planning and woody biomass harvesting, soil element cycling, and the molecular biology and genetic engineering of trees
- Processes for biochemical and thermal conversion of biomass, including chemical pretreatment and enzymatic hydrolysis of cellulose, fermentation, product purification, and enzyme/microorganism improvement
- Bioprocessing facility location, harvesting, logistics, and community-related issues
- Developing, adapting, and testing engines and other system components to utilize ethanol, biodiesel, and other bio-products
- Technology evaluation and appraisal of commercialization potential
- Environmental assessment of the life cycle of biofuel production and usage and comparison with conventional alternatives

The presentation will summarize the activities associated with the Wood-to-Wheels initiative and describe the potential benefits that are achievable.

KEY WORDS: biofuels, sustainability, wood-to-wheels, value chain

*Corresponding author: Michigan Technological University, Department of Chemical Engineering and Sustainable Futures Institute, 1400 Townsend Drive, Houghton, MI 49931; Phone: (906) 487-3468; Email: drshonna@mtu.edu

GENETICS OF YIELD AND BIOMASS COMPOSITION OF SHRUB WILLOW BIOENERGY CROPS BRED AND SELECTED IN NORTH AMERICA

Lawrence B. Smart*, Michelle J. Serapiglia, Kimberly D. Cameron, Arthur J. Stipanovic, Timothy A. Volk, and Lawrence P. Abrahamson

College of Environmental Science and Forestry, State University of New York

Fast-growing shrub willow is a proven bioenergy crop in Europe and is being adopted commercially in regions of North America. Breeding and selection of shrub willows adapted for field conditions in North America have been conducted at SUNY's College of Environmental Science and Forestry since 1998. From more than 2,000 individuals produced through breeding in 1998 and 1999, a number have been selected for improved biomass yield in two field trials with small, replicated plots. A comparison of first- and second-rotation yield results from these trials will be presented, demonstrating that the yield of a number of varieties exceeded that of the best current production variety, 'SV1'. The highest mean yield in these small plots was 40 percent higher than that of 'SV1', which typically yields 4 to 5 dry tons ac^{-1} yr^{-1}. A selected number of these high-yielding varieties have been scaled-up and planted in yield trials established using production-style spacing on several sites in the United States, Canada, and Northern Ireland to evaluate yield potential across a range of environmental conditions. To encourage commercial deployment, seven varieties were patented and have been licensed to a nursery for commercial scale-up and sale of planting stock. Current and future work is focused on characterizing the genetic basis for differences in biomass composition among diverse high-yielding varieties. High-resolution thermogravimetric analysis has been used to characterize the chemical composition of biomass harvested from more than 100 varieties in the SUNY-ESF breeding program. Initial characterization of willow genes encoding key enzymes in lignin, cellulose, and hemicellulose biosynthesis will be presented.

KEY WORDS: cellulose, lignin, molecular biology, *Salix*, thermogravimetric analysis, wood composition

*Corresponding author: State University of New York, College of Environmental Science and Forestry, Department of Environmental and Forest Biology, 246 Illick Hall, Syracuse, NY 13210; Phone: (315) 470-6737; Fax: (315) 470-6934; Email: lbsmart@esf.edu

SOCIALLY RESPONSIBLE EXPANSION OF BRAZILIAN ETHANOL

Gerd Sparovek[a,*], Rodrigo Maule[b], and Göran Berndes[c]

[a]*University of São Paulo, Brazil*
[b]*Entropix Engenharia, Brazil*
[c]*Chalmers University, Sweden*

Because of increasing demand, Brazil is expected to expand its sugarcane-based ethanol production. Addressing concerns about social impacts of such an expansion requires careful consideration of the complexity of Brazilian agriculture. In a conventional expansion scenario, mills tend to cluster and sugarcane displaces most land-use types, thus dominating the landscape regionally. This pattern may impact expansion areas by relocating traditional small holders or withdrawing them from agricultural production, competing with food production, concentrating land property because of land market dynamization, reducing agro-ecosystem diversity, and displacing extensive beef cattle or milk production. This process will change social and economic structures dramatically, and probably will create negative externalities. Integration of sugarcane production with the prevailing land uses in expansion areas is key to reducing the impacts of displacement, and to preserving food production and the established social and economic environment. This paper examines integration pathways for livestock and food crop production, using both the potential of the industrial process for improving livestock production and the coexistence of food crops in sugarcane fields. Livestock production may be intensified and integrated using industrial residues for feed production, resulting in the maintenance of current production levels on a substantially smaller area. Food production also can be improved, to some extent, using areas where sugarcane will be renewed. As a result of these integration pathways, sugarcane production potential is not affected substantially, and social externalities are mitigated by allowing sugarcane production to coexist with livestock and food crop production.

KEY WORDS: sugarcane, Brazil, expansion, sustainability

*Corresponding author: University of São Paulo, Soil Science Department, Av. Pádua Dias, 11, CEP 13.418-900, Piracicaba (SP), Brazil; Phone: +55 19 3429 4503; Email: gerd@usp.br

*** INVITED SPEAKER ***

GENETIC IMPROVEMENT OF HYBRID POPLAR FOR THE RENEWABLE FUELS INDUSTRY: A PACIFIC NORTHWEST PERSPECTIVE

Brian J. Stanton[a],*, Jon D. Johnson[b], and David B. Neale[c]

[a]*GreenWood Resources*
[b]*Washington State Universtiy*
[c]*University of California, Davis*

More than 14,000 hectares of poplar plantations are being managed in the Pacific Northwest by the pulp and paper, timber, and the environmental-services industries. The success of these operations has been due in large measure to the availability of highly selected, elite plant material of superior growth and adaptability, the selection of which has been tailored to three main criteria: 1) compatibility with plantation management practices (e.g., ease of clonal propagation, rapid growth, pest resistance, good stem form); 2) adaptability to local climatic and edaphic conditions; and 3) suitability of wood and fiber properties for paper and lumber manufacture (e.g., wood specific gravity, fiber length, cell wall thickness). Poplar is now being considered as a priority feedstock for the cellulosic liquid fuels industry. Whether it contributes to the Northwest's future renewable energy portfolio will depend upon the availability of cultivars of high biomass productivity coupled with high rates of conversion within specific liquid fuels production processes. Two approaches are being used in breeding new *Populus* energy varieties. First, variation in wood specific gravity, calorific value, and carbohydrate and lignin chemistry is being quantified in advance of a revised hybridization plan for feedstock improvement in the *P.* × *canadensis* and *P.* × *generosa* taxa. Secondly, molecular tools are being developed to identify DNA sequence variation in genes underlying phenotypic variation in cellulose quantity, quality, and extractability in *P. trichocarpa* and *P. nigra* breeding populations. The focus of both approaches is the design of a genomics-assisted hybridization program for a new class of energy cultivars, the biomass of which will be competitive with other cellulosic feedstocks when measured on the basis of the price per unit of delivered carbohydrate and the ease of conversion to liquid fuels.

KEY WORDS: genetic improvement, wood chemistry, *Populus*, renewable energy, genomics

*Corresponding author: 121 S.W. Salmon Street, Suite 1020, Portland, OR 97204; Phone: (971) 533-7052; Email: bstanton@greenwoodresources.com

*** **INVITED SPEAKER** ***

IRRIGATION EFFECTS IN A COTTONWOOD PLANTATION IN THE LOWER MISSISSIPPI RIVER ALLUVIAL VALLEY

H. Christoph Stuhlinger[a],*, Paul F. Doruska[b], and Matthew H. Pelkki[c]

[a]Division of Agriculture, University of Arkansas
[b]College of Natural Resources, University of Wisconsin – Stevens Point
[c]University of Arkansas-Monticello, School of Forest Resources

Eastern cottonwood (*Populus deltoides* Bartr.) may have potential as a short-rotation alternate crop on marginal farmlands in the U.S. South to meet increasing biomass demands for pulp and bioenergy applications. This 10-year study, installed in the Delta region of Arkansas, investigated the effects of irrigation on the growth of nine cottonwood clones (five Stoneville clones, two Texas clones, and two hybrid clones). Survival, height, diameter, and biomass production of the cottonwoods were compared between the irrigated-bedded treatment and the unirrigated-subsoiled treatment, and among the nine clones. Poor initial survival caused the replanting of several clones the second year and the separate analysis of the two groups of clones. Survival for some clones dropped off greatly after 5 years. The irrigated-bedding treatment increased volume growth (biomass production) over the unirrigated-subsoiled treatment, and for some clones, irrigation more than doubled volume growth. Lower survival resulted in more growing space and greater volume growth for some clones. Overall, irrigation increased height, diameter, and volume growth of all clones except one. The best clonal biomass production was 2.1 dry tons/acre/year in the unirrigated treatment and 4.3 dry tons/acre/year in the irrigated treatment, both less than expected. Some clones produced more biomass during the first 5 years than the second 5 years. Economic considerations require the additional investigation of growing selected clones in the Delta under various spacing, rotation length, and cultural treatment regimes to determine if cottonwood can be a competitive woody crop in this region.

KEY WORDS: biomass production, eastern cottonwood, plantation, clones

*Corresponding author: University of Arkansas-Monticello, School of Forest Resources, P.O. Box 3468, Monticello, AR 71656-3468; Phone: (870) 460-1749; Email: stuhlinger@uamont.edu

ECOLOGICAL ASPECTS OF CELLULOSIC BIOMASS SUPPLY FROM WHOLE-TREE CHIPPING AND SLASH REMOVAL

Philip A. Tappe*, Matthew H. Pelkki, Robert L. Ficklin, and Hal O. Liechty

Arkansas Forest Resources Center, University of Arkansas

Currently, corn and soybean are the primary feedstocks producing ethanol and biodiesel, respectively. However, it is unlikely that these crops will be sufficient to meet biofuel demands, particularly since they are also important food sources. Cellulosic ethanol has the potential to replace 30 percent of U.S. petroleum use. The collection of post-logging forest residues, or logging slash, is a vital component of a cellulosic biomass supply for biofuel production. Pine plantations produce the majority of harvested forest volume in the U.S. South and are projected to increase 53 percent in area by 2050. Projections estimate that two-thirds of the national softwood harvest will occur on plantations, which cover 20 percent of the U.S. forest base. Clearly, pine plantations have an important role in producing biofuel feedstocks. However, whole-tree chipping (i.e., removal of all above-stump biomass) may have deleterious impacts on site productivity and ecosystem services with the removal of high amounts of logging slash. Forest harvesting can reduce the base saturation of soils, and this reduction intensifies with the amount of biomass removed. Whole-tree harvesting also can reduce cycling of soil carbon, thus modifying soil properties and reducing future productivity. The quantity, size, distribution, and decay status of woody debris in forests influence plant and animal community composition and diversity. However, removal of logging slash has the potential to negatively impact several species groups. We summarize current knowledge regarding environmental dimensions of whole-tree chipping and logging slash removal in the U.S. South and identify critical information gaps related to sustainable cellulosic biomass supply.

KEY WORDS: biodiversity, harvesting, nutrient cycling, slash, soil carbon, woody debris

*Corresponding author: University of Arkansas, Arkansas Forest Resources Center & School of Forest Resources, P.O. Box 3468, Monticello, AR 71656-3468; Phone: (870) 460-1352; Email: tappe@uamont.edu

CANOPY STRUCTURE, LIGHT INTERCEPTION, AND LIGHT-USE EFFICIENCY IN WILLOW

Pradeep J. Tharakan, Timothy A. Volk, Chris A. Nowak, and Godfrey J. Ofezu*

College of Environmental Science and Forestry, State University of New York

According to the light-use efficiency model, differential biomass production among willow clones may be attributed to either the differences in the amount of light intercepted, or the efficiency with which the intercepted light is converted to aboveground biomass, or both. We tested this model on a second-rotation willow coppice in its first growing season at an existing genetic selection trial at Tully, NY. We investigated the variation in aboveground biomass production (AGBP) in relation to the percent incoming radiation intercepted ($IPAR_F$) and light-use efficiency (ε) for five willow clones grown in a short-rotation woody crop (SRWC) system. The study was conducted during a 2-month period (June 15 to August 15, 2001) when growing conditions were deemed most favorable. The objectives were to: (1) assess the relative importance of $IPAR_F$ in explaining variation in AGBP; and (2) identify the key drivers of variation in ε from a suite of measured leaf and canopy-level traits. We hypothesized that variation in AGBP would be more closely related to $IPAR_F$ than ε and that ε variation would be closely related to traits that maximized canopy photosynthesis. AGBP varied nearly threefold among genotypes (3.55 to 10.02 Mg ha^{-1}), while ε spanned a twofold range (1.21 to 2.52 g MJ^{-1}). At peak leaf area index (LAI), $IPAR_F$ ranged from 66 percent to 92 percent. Nonetheless, AGBP was strongly related to $IPAR_F$ and ε. An additive model combining photosynthesis on leaf area basis, leaf mass per unit area, and light extinction coefficient produced the most compelling predictors of ε. The results suggest that in a post-coppice willow, the ability to maximize $IPAR_F$ and ε early in the growing season is advantageous for maximizing biomass production. From these clonal differences, productivity and yield improvements can be achieved by selection of superior genotypes in the short-rotation coppice system.

KEY WORDS: aboveground biomass, *Salix* sp., short-rotation woody crops

*Corresponding author: State University of New York, College of Environmental Science and Forestry, 241 Illick Hall, 1 Forestry Drive, Syracuse, NY 13210; Phone: (315) 470-6774/4742; Email:gjofezu@syr.edu

BUILDING A CELLULOSIC BIOFUELS INDUSTRY FROM THE GROUND UP: TENNESSEE BIOFUELS INITIATIVE

Kelly Tiller

The University of Tennessee, Institute of Agriculture, Office of Bioenergy Programs

Tennessee is leading an ambitious effort to develop a cellulosic biofuels industry. With more than $300 million in state, federal, and private funding dedicated to the effort, Tennessee is poised to succeed. The Tennessee Biofuels Initiative is led by the University of Tennessee, Institute of Agriculture, with partners including the Oak Ridge National Laboratory and other third-party private sector technology partners. The centerpiece of the effort is construction and operation of a 10 percent scale (2 to 4 million gallons per year) cellulosic biorefinery, supplied by locally grown switchgrass and wood chips. While the research-oriented demonstration-scale biorefinery is the heart of the Initiative, key to the entire project is the focus on developing a supply chain for providing sufficient, reliable, and sustainable dedicated energy crop feedstocks. The Initiative is focused largely on working with local farmers (within a 50-mile radius of the biorefinery) to develop switchgrass as a feedstock supply chain, and provides more than $12 million for research, extension, education, and direct incentive payments for participating farmers to plant up to 8,000 acres of switchgrass. The integrated project is designed to answer a variety of research questions, ranging from feedstock supply systems to pretreatment and conversion technology approaches to industrial processing and scale-up to systems for product distribution and marketing. The University of Tennessee has contracted with local farmers to plant more than 700 acres of switchgrass in 2008, with significant related research under way in the areas of agronomics, production management, harvest systems, storage, and transportation. The biorefinery is scheduled to be operational by the second quarter of 2010. The integrated systems approach of the Biofuels Initiative is designed to foster development of a large-scale commercial biofuels industry in Tennessee and the region.

KEY WORDS: cellulosic biofuels, sustainable energy crop feedstock, switchgrass, farmer incentive program, biorefinery, conversion technology for marketing and distribution

*Contact information: Director of External Operations, The University of Tennessee, Institute of Agriculture, Office of Bioenergy Programs, 2506 Jacob Drive, Knoxville, TN 37996-4570; Phone: (865) 946-1130; Email: ktiller@tennessee.edu

POPLAR AND WILLOW SHORT ROTATION INTENSIVE CULTURE (SRIC) CROPS IN WESTERN CANADA

Cees ("Case") van Oosten

SilviConsult Woody Crops Technology Inc.

An overview will be presented of poplar and willow short-rotation intensive-culture (SRIC) crops in western Canada. Western Canada consists of the Prairie Provinces (Manitoba, Saskatchewan, and Alberta) and British Columbia. These crops are grown or have potential in four distinctive crop zones, each with its particular challenges. South-central Manitoba is in a similar crop zone as Minnesota and southern Ontario; southeastern Manitoba, Saskatchewan, and Alberta and the northeast Peace region of British Columbia are in a distinct crop zone, typified by the transition between prairie grasslands and the boreal forest region. In British Columbia one crop zone parallels the Coast Mountain range on the Westside; the second zone is wedged between the Coast Mountain range in the west and the Rocky Mountains in the east.

Although poplars have been planted for a long time in the Prairie Provinces in farm shelterbelts, the concept of SRIC hybrid poplar crops is relatively new. SRIC willow crops are very new to the region and are all experimental in nature. This presentation will discuss the challenges and potential of these crop systems in this region. In coastal British Columbia the culture of poplars has a long and successful history; however, the region has been subjected to various ups and downs in SRIC hybrid poplar crop systems that had more to do with corporate directions than with the crop itself. To date there has been little activity with SRIC willow crops in British Columbia.

KEY WORDS: hybrid poplar, *Populus*, willow, *Salix*

*Contact information: 2356 York Crescent, Nanaimo, BC V9T 4N3, Canada; Phone: (250) 758-8230; Email: silviconsult@telus.net

*** INVITED SPEAKER ***

WOOD BIOENERGY SYSTEMS IN CANADA

Ken C.J. Van Rees

Department of Soil Science, University of Saskatchewan

The development of woody short-rotation intensive-culture (SRIC) biomass productions systems is just beginning in Canada and presents a unique opportunity to engage farmers in growing a different crop. Bioenergy production systems are feasible in Canada but will depend on selecting the right clones that are suitable to our climate zones and soils but that also produce satisfactory yields. Whether these systems can be sustainable in the long term is still uncertain as we have no trials to evaluate potential long-term productivity and nutrient cycling; however, current research suggests that fertilization may not be necessary in the short term when plantations are established on agricultural land. Among the obstacles for producer involvement in bioenergy systems is first of all changing the farmer mindset that growing a crop for longer than 1 year is not an impediment to earning money. At one time or another, most farmers in the prairies have removed woody biomass on their farms to increase their capacity for growing crops and are reluctant to go back into "woody" systems. However, the newer generation of farmers may be less reluctant to do so because of an ability to take more risks, a greater environmental consciousness and better education. High initial establishment costs (>$10,000/ha) may also deter producers from participating in woody biomass systems without government incentives or other mechanisms to reduce up-front establishment costs. Finally, having a stable, growing industry that can utilize this material is essential in order for producers to see the value in committing to growing woody biomass for the long term.

KEY WORDS: woody biomass, farmer perceptions, sustainability

*Contact information: University of Saskatchewan, 51 Campus Drive, Saskatoon, SK, S7N 5A8, Canada; Phone: (306) 966-6853; Email: ken.vanrees@usask.ca

*** INVITED SPEAKER ***

REGIONAL SITE-SELECTION MODELS FOR HYBRID POPLARS

Robert C. Venette*, Michael E. Ostry, and Kathleen M. Ward

U.S. Forest Service, Northern Research Station

Hybrid poplars (*Populus* spp.) can quickly produce significant biomass compared with other hardwood species and, as a result, are increasingly being grown for pulp and wood products. Global energy demands have rekindled interest in hybrid poplar as an alternative, renewable energy source. Future production of hybrid poplar to meet demand will depend on optimization of site selection, clone selection, and management practices. In this study, we attempt to identify and validate site factors that are correlated with growth potential of hybrid poplar. Because data were unavailable to describe the growth of common clones replicated over a range of sites, we selected aspen (*P. tremuloides*) as a surrogate poplar species. We identified 306 aspen stands that were naturally growing in near-monocultures at densities comparable to those recommended for commercial hybrid poplar production. We then used ridge-regression to evaluate the relationship between aspen site index and several soil and climatological measures. Site index was positively correlated with the percentage (by weight) of coarse soil particles and negatively correlated with calcium carbonate concentration, vertical water flow, and hardwood habitat quality. To validate the model, in 2005 and 2006 we measured diameter at breast height (d.b.h.) of *P. deltoides* × *nigra* and *P. nigra* × *maximowiczii* clones in 31 commercial plantations in Todd County, Minnesota, planted in 1999 and 2000. Observed d.b.h. was positively correlated with predicted site index for plantings in 2000 but not 1999, presumably because of outbreaks of defoliating insects. Our resulting map may be helpful when selecting future sites for hybrid poplar plantations, but clone selection, insect and disease impacts, and management practices have as much or greater impact on fiber production.

KEY WORDS: *Populus*, productivity, site relationships

*Corresponding author: Northern Research Station, 1561 Lindig St., St. Paul, MN 55108; Phone: (651) 649-5028; Email: rvenette@fs.fed.us

DEVELOPMENT OF SWITCHGRASS INTO A BIOMASS ENERGY CROP

Kenneth Vogel*, Rob Mitchell, and Gautam Sarath

USDA Agricultural Research Service, Grain, Forage, and Bioenergy Research Unit

Switchgrass (*Panicum virgatum* L.) is a North American prairie grass that is being developed into a biomass energy crop in the United States and other countries. Research on switchgrass as a pasture and forage crop was initiated in the mid-1930s in a USDA and University of Nebraska cooperative program. In 1990, breeding and management research also was initiated to develop switchgrass into a biomass energy crop. Critical questions for a biomass/bioenergy production system include: What are the economics? Is energy from biomass net energy-positive? Is production system information available and verified? Is the system sustainable? To address these questions, 10 farmers in the mid-continental United States were contracted to grow switchgrass in 6-8 ha fields for a 5-year period and manage it as a biomass energy crop using available cultivars and management practices from 2000 to 2005. Results indicate that during this period switchgrass biomass feedstock could have been produced in this region at a cost of about \$50 Mg^{-1} at the farm gate, which translates to about \$0.13 per liter of ethanol. Net energy yield on the established switchgrass fields was 60 GJ ha^{-1} y^{-1}. In these farmer trials, switchgrass produced 540 percent more renewable energy than nonrenewable energy consumed. These baseline studies represent the technology that was available for switchgrass in 2000 and 2001 when the fields were planted but clearly demonstrate that for switchgrass a full array of production system technology is available for its use as a biomass energy crop. Improved genetics and agronomics will further enhance energy sustainability and biofuel yield of switchgrass. Carbon sequestration research is still in progress, but the initial results are very encouraging. Technology has been developed to rotate from switchgrass to crops including maize and soybeans and back to switchgrass without plowing.

KEY WORDS: herbaceous perennials, switchgrass, genetics, feedstocks

*Corresponding author: University of Nebraska-Lincoln, 314 Biochemistry Hall, Lincoln, NE 68583; Phone: (402) 472-1564; Email: ken.vogel@ars.usda.gov

*** INVITED SPEAKER ***

ILLINOIS STUDIES OF *MISCANTHUS* × *GIGANTEUS* FOR BIOMASS FEEDSTOCK PRODUCTION

Tom Voigt

University of Illinois

While switchgrass (*Panicum virgatum*) is considered to be the primary biomass feedstock for many portions of the United States, another biomass-producing grass, *Miscanthus* × *giganteus* (*M.* × *g.*), deserves consideration. Originating in Japan, *M.* × *g.* has been used for many years as a landscape plant in the United States, but since 2002, it has been the subject of University of Illinois research interest because of its potentially great biomass production. For more than 15 years, the grass has been studied and grown in Europe where its senescent stems are harvested and burned to produce heat and electricity. *Miscanthus* × *giganteus* is a perennial, warm-season grass native to Asia. It is a reproductively sterile hybrid believed to have *Miscanthus sinensis* and *M. sacchariflorus* as its parents. *M.* × *g.* begins growth in April and typically reaches 2 m by the end of May in central Illinois. Growth continues throughout the summer, and it normally grows taller than 4 m by the end of September. It is propagated asexually using plantlets produced in tissue culture or by rhizome divisions. Following field planting, *M.* × *g.* generally takes at least three growing seasons to become fully established and reach optimal biomass production. In Illinois, the senesced stems can be harvested from early December through early March. As an example of its prolific biomass production, annual dry-matter *M.* × *g.* yields from University of Illinois research plots planted in 2002 and averaged over 2004, 2005, and 2006 produced 22.0 t ha^{-1}, 34.7 t ha^{-1}, and 35.4 t ha^{-1} in northern, central, and southern Illinois, respectively. In this presentation, Illinois research findings that include evaluations of greenhouse and field propagation of *M.* × *g.* rhizomes and rhizome harvesting and planting methods will be shared. The tolerance of *M.* × *g.* to pre- and post-emergence herbicides used to control grassy and broadleaf weeds in new plantings also will be discussed. Finally, this presentation will explore past Illinois agronomic experiences and the realistic opportunities for future expansion of this crop.

KEY WORDS: bioenergy, herbaceous perennial, sterile hybrid

*Contact information: University of Illinois, S-416 Turner Hall, 1102 South Goodwin Ave, Urbana, IL 61801; Email: tvoigt@uiuc.edu

*** INVITED SPEAKER ***

COMMERCIALIZING WILLOW BIOMASS CROPS FOR BIOENERGY AND BIOPRODUCTS IN THE NORTHEASTERN AND MIDWESTERN UNITED STATES

Timothy A. Volk[a,*], Lawrence P. Abrahamson[a], Thomas E. Amidon[a], Daniel J. Aneshansley[b], Kimberly D. Cameron[a], Gregg A. Johnson[c], John Posselius[d], Dennis Rak[e], Lawrence B. Smart[a], Eric Spomer[f], and Edwin H. White[a]

[a]State University of New York, College of Environmental Science and Forestry
[b]Dept. of Biological and Environmental Engineering, Cornell University
[c]Southern Research and Outreach Center, University of Minnesota
[d]Case New Holland America, LLC
[e]Double A Willow
[f]Catalyst Renewables

Interest in the commercial production of willow biomass crops has developed rapidly due to changes in prices of fossil fuels, concerns about energy security, and growing pressure to address issues related to global climate change. Several bottlenecks to commercialization are being addressed, including the production of willow planting stock at Double A Willow in western New York and a new harvesting system being developed in conjunction with Case New Holland. Catalyst Renewables installed the first commercial willow acreage in North America in the spring of 2006 and has a goal of establishing several thousand acres over the next few years. At the market end the first commercial-scale test of willow biomass crops in North America is under way at the Lyonsdale Biomass combined heat and power (CHP) plant in upstate New York with several thousand tons of willow biomass. Several other power and CHP projects as well as small-scale heating projects are being developed with willow as a component of the feedstock. Two pilot wood-based biorefineries are being built in upstate New York and willow has been successfully tested in both of these processes as well as several other conversion processes.

Modification of the Conservation Reserve Program and the Conservation Reserve Enhancement Program, the federal biomass tax credit for closed-loop biomass, and the New York Renewable Portfolio Standard have all placed value on some of the environmental and rural development benefits associated with willow biomass crops. The combination of these improvements has created a solid foundation for the commercialization of willow biomass crops in the northeast and midwest United States. However, there is a lack of experience with the establishment and management of willow biomass crops at a commercial scale. To avoid large-scale failures or disappointing production early in the development of the crop, an ongoing outreach and research program to support the commercialization is being conducted.

KEY WORDS: Salix, short-rotation woody crops, willow harvesting systems, biorefinery

*Corresponding author: State University of New York, College of Environmental Science and Forestry, Department of Forest and Natural Resources Management, 346 Illick Hall, 1 Forestry Drive, Syracuse, NY 13210; Phone: (315) 470-6774; Email: tavolk@esf.edu

*** INVITED SPEAKER ***

EVALUATING EFFLUENT AND CANAL WATER IRRIGATION FOR WOOD BIOMASS PRODUCTION AND PHYTOTECHNOLOGY

N. Larry White

Saskatchewan Forest Centre

Irrigation provides an opportunity to produce increased volumes of wood biomass and identify phytotechnology applications. There are currently up to 500,000 underutilized irrigable acres in the irrigation area of Saskatchewan where woody crops could be grown. If landowners are to grow biomass tree crops in the future, there must be a positive economic return. The unknown is the potential yield of various tree crops under dryland and irrigation management systems. Projects are under way to evaluate the yields of hybrid poplar, willow, and various other tree species using secondary cell effluent water and clear canal water from the Saskatchewan River. These projects will help to identify those species which do well under irrigation and will identify future genetic improvement needs under an irrigation regime. The two sources of water are being used to evaluate the performance of two different types of irrigation systems: a) a trickle system and b) a microsprinkler system. In addition three different systems will be used to determine soil moisture levels, which in turn will determine the application rates for irrigation water. The projects will help communities better understand the technology involved in using irrigation to dispense with effluent water in an environmentally safe manner. More than 100 communities in the Province could potentially benefit from this technology. A secondary benefit of using trees to dispose of the effluent water is the production of a marketable wood product. The projects will further demonstrate to communities the use of trees for phytotechnology applications.

KEY WORDS: irrigation, phytotechnology, effluent management, hybrid poplar, willow

*Contact information: 101-1061 Central Avenue, Prince Albert, SK, S6V 6K7, Canada; E mail: lwhite@saskforestcentre.ca

A COMPARATIVE COST ANALYSIS OF LOGISTICS FOR HERBACEOUS ENERGY CROPS AND SHORT-ROTATION WOODY CROPS

Erin G. Wilkerson*, Robert D. Perlack, and Anthony F. Turhollow

Oak Ridge National Laboratory

Mandates requiring the use of cellulosic and other advanced biofuels in coming years will establish a demand for dedicated energy crops in addition to residues from agriculture and forestry. Primary energy crop candidates fall into one of two categories: herbaceous crops and short-rotation woody crops. Supply chains for woody crops and herbaceous crops vary in the way that the feedstocks are processed, handled, and stored. Herbaceous energy crops, such as switchgrass, are typically harvested as bales and stored under cover (in a building or tarped) until the material is needed. The bales are delivered to the biorefinery, where they are chopped before being loaded into the reactor. Woody crops, on the other hand, are harvested as needed and chipped at the landing prior to transport to the biorefinery. In this system, handling is minimized and long-term storage of woody materials, other than that required at the biorefinery, is not needed. The objective of this paper is to compare the logistics costs of short-rotation woody crops to herbaceous energy crops. The comparison will include harvesting, forwarding or staging to the landing or farmgate, chipping or packaging, handling, storage, hauling, and unloading at a biorefinery. The effects of yield, which vary by region, on logistics costs will be included in the analysis. The results of this analysis will be useful in identifying areas of improvement in supply-chain logistics and for assisting the cellulosic industry in identifying the best energy crop for various situations.

KEY WORDS: logistics, economics, short-rotation, woody crops, switchgrass

*Corresponding author: Oak Ridge National Laboratory, Environmental Sciences Division, P.O. Box 2008, Building 1062, Oak Ridge, TN 37831; Phone: (865) 576-4814; Email: wilkersoneg@ornl.gov

MULTIPLE CRITERIA DECIDING ON PHYTOREMEDIATION OF A HEAVY METAL CONTAMINATED AGRICULTURAL AREA CASE: THE CAMPINE, BELGIUM

Nele Witters*, Ann Ruttens, and Theo Thewys

Hasselt University, Centre for Environmental Sciences

From the end of the 19th century until the mid 1970s, zinc and lead were refined at several locations in the northeastern Belgium using a pyrometallurgical process. Consequently, a large area (280 km²) is moderately contaminated from atmospheric deposition of the dust, with lead (Pb), zinc (Zn), and cadmium (Cd) being the main pollutants. These heavy metals can be found in the upper layer of the soil (30 to 40 cm). Large areas of land in the region are currently in agricultural use, but soils and crops often exceed legal Cd limits. Regional policy therefore prescribes that the soils should be remediated, but at the same time it is desirable to keep the income of the farmers constant. One possible way to achieve both goals is the use of phytoremediation in combination with the growth of energy crops (e.g. energy maize, rapeseed, and woody species). This approach brings us to the concept of a multifunctional biomass system. Society's acceptance of phytoremediation is determined by the effect it has on farmer income. This income could be supported by producing renewable energy (heat and electricity) from the polluted biomass. The goal of this study is to compare the different crops on their remediating, economic, ecological, and energy impacts (criteria). Monte Carlo analysis shows the sensitivity of the economic viability to regional subsidising systems (due to high costs involved in converting the polluted biomass into energy and in processing the waste) and to energy crop prices. Preliminary results of our study show that when a high weight is attributed to the economic perspective, calculations do (for now) not favor short-rotation woody crops over large biomass-producing crops like energy maize. If, however, a larger weight is given to phytoremediation capacities, results give an advantage to woody crops.

KEY WORDS: agriculture, woody crops, phytoremediation, economics

*Corresponding author: Hasselt University, Centre for Environmental Sciences, Faculty of Applied Economic Sciences, Department of Economics-Law, Agoralaan – Gebouw D, 3590 Diepenbeek, Belgium; Phone: +32 11 26 87 57; Fax: +32 11 26 87 60, Email: nele.witters@uhasselt.be

POPULUS ROOT SYSTEM MORPHOLOGY DURING PHYTOREMEDIATION OF LANDFILL LEACHATE

Jill A. Zalesny[a,*], Ronald S. Zalesny, Jr.[a], David R. Coyle[b], Richard B. Hall[c], and Edmund O. Bauer[a]

[a]*U.S. Forest Service, Northern Research Station, Institute for Applied Ecosystem Studies*
[b]*Department of Entomology, University of Wisconsin*
[c]*Department of Natural Resource Ecology and Management, Iowa State University*

Using *Populus* for phytoremediation of wastewaters, including landfill leachate, is necessary in North America because of increased municipal solid waste generation. *Populus* species and hybrids are ideal for such applications because of their high water usage rates, fast growth, and extensive root systems. Adventitious rooting (i.e., lateral rooting from primordia and basal rooting from callus) of *Populus* is important for phytotechnologies to ensure successful plantation establishment with genotypes that thrive when irrigated with highly variable or specific contaminants. We evaluated differences in root system morphology following establishment with high-salinity municipal solid waste landfill leachate or uncontaminated well water (control). *Populus* clones (NC13460, NC14018, NC14104, NC14106, DM115, DN5, NM2, NM6) were irrigated during 2005 and 2006 in northern Wisconsin and tested for differences in morphology of lateral and basal root types, as well as fine (0 to 2 mm), small (2 to 5 mm), and coarse (> 5 mm) roots. Across treatments and clones, trees averaged 5 roots per root type. Leachate-irrigated trees had 88 percent (lateral) and 106 percent (basal) more roots than those irrigated with water, yet the leachate:water ratio for number of basal roots ranged from 0.5 (NM2) to 2.5 (NC13460). Presence of fine roots with leachate was 97 percent of water irrigation, while trees with leachate had 113 percent (small) and 90 percent (coarse) as many roots versus water. The leachate:water ratio for number of lateral and basal coarse roots ranged from 0.4 (NC14018) to 1.2 (NC14106, NM2) and 0.5 (DM115) to 2.7 (NC14104), respectively. Despite root necrosis and regrowth in 23 percent of the trees, leachate irrigation did not negatively affect root diameter or dry mass ($P > 0.05$). Given that adequate rooting is necessary for plantation establishment, leachate and similar wastewaters are viable irrigation and fertilization sources of *Populus* crops used as feedstocks for biofuels, bioenergy, and bioproducts.

KEY WORDS: poplar genetics, phytotechnologies, tree improvement, waste management, adventitious rooting

*Corresponding author: U.S. Forest Service, Northern Research Station, 5985 Highway K, Rhinelander, WI 54501; Phone: (715) 362-1111; Email: jzalesny@fs.fed.us

POTENTIAL CHLORIDE AND SODIUM UPTAKE FOR 2- TO 11-YEAR-OLD *POPULUS* IRRIGATED WITH LANDFILL LEACHATE IN THE NORTH CENTRAL UNITED STATES

Jill A. Zalesny* and Ronald S. Zalesny, Jr.

U.S. Forest Service, Northern Research Station, Institute for Applied Ecosystem Studies

In the north central United States, regulators and resource managers need information about wastewater-applied chloride (Cl^-) and sodium (Na^+), as well as the response to these salts of *Populus* genotypes grown over an entire rotation. In this study, we have combined our 2-year establishment biomass and salt uptake field data with previously published regional field test biomass data to estimate uptake potential and field-scale application thresholds for years 2 to 11 of a *Populus* rotation. Our objective was to estimate uptake of Cl^- and Na^+ throughout a rotation, with emphasis on developmental stages that tolerate increased application rates of high-salinity irrigation without environmental consequence. Mid-rotation projected uptake was stable for years 2 and 3 but increased from years 3 to 6. Estimated cumulative uptake was maximized during year 6 when clonal responses ranged from 22 to 175 kg Cl^- ha^{-1} yr^{-1} and 8 to 74 kg Na^+ ha^{-1} yr^{-1}. The estimated annual uptake for clones was highly variable and dependent on specific clone × site interactions. Annual uptake during year 6 ranged from 8 to 54 kg Cl^- ha^{-1} yr^{-1} and 3 to 23 kg Na^+ ha^{-1} yr^{-1}. Full-rotation plantation uptake mirrored mean annual growth in forest trees with the greatest projected uptake during 4 to 9 years (Cl^-) and 4 to 8 years (Na^+). Annual uptake was maximized during year six for Cl^- (32 kg ha^{-1} yr^{-1}) and Na^+ (13 kg ha^{-1} yr^{-1}) when peak accumulation was 2.7 times greater than year 11. We present salt uptake estimates along with stages of plantation development that are conducive to variable Cl^- and Na^+ application and that are necessary for decision-making required by regulators, resource managers, and researchers who must achieve regulatory compliance while maintaining ecological sustainability.

KEY WORDS: salt accumulation, poplar, wastewater recycling, sustainable forestry, short-rotation woody crops

*Corresponding author: U.S. Forest Service, Northern Research Station, 5985 Highway K, Rhinelander, WI 54501; Phone: (715) 362-1111; Email: jzalesny@fs.fed.us

BIOMASS POTENTIAL OF *POPULUS* IN THE MIDWESTERN UNITED STATES

Ronald S. Zalesny, Jr.[a,*], Richard B. Hall[b], Jill A. Zalesny[a], William E. Berguson[c], Bernard G. McMahon[c], and Glen R. Stanosz[d]

[a]*U.S. Forest Service, Northern Research Station, Institute for Applied Ecosystem Studies*
[b]*Department of Natural Resource Ecology and Management, Iowa State University*
[c]*Natural Resources Research Institute, University of Minnesota - Duluth*
[d]*Department of Plant Pathology, University of Wisconsin*

The use of *Populus* feedstock for biofuels, bioenergy, and bioproducts is becoming economically feasible as global fossil fuel prices increase. Maximizing biomass production from *Populus* plantations deployed across regional landscapes largely depends on recognizing and evaluating genotype × environment interactions, given broad genetic variation among *Populus* genotypes at strategic (genomic group) and operational (clone) levels. A network of *Populus* regional field tests was established in the Midwest in 1995, 1997, and 2000 to assess productivity of 190 clones grown at Westport, MN (45.7 °N, 95.2 °W), Waseca, MN (only 2000; 44.1 °N, 93.5 °W), Arlington, WI (43.3 °N, 89.4 °W), and Ames, IA (42.0 °N, 93.6 °W). We evaluated biomass production potential of these genotypes throughout plantation development and identified specific clones with yield substantially greater than current commercial controls (Eugenei, NM6). Biomass production of the best six clones in Ames ranged from 1.9 to 2.4 (4 yrs), 5.0 to 9.3 (7 yrs), and 6.4 to 10.9 tons ac^{-1} yr^{-1} (9 yrs), while ranges at Arlington were 2.3 to 3.2 (3 yrs), 6.6 to 9.3 (6 yrs), and 7.2 to 9.4 tons ac^{-1} yr^{-1} (8 yrs). Biomass of the best six clones at Westport ranged from 1.0 to 1.7 (5 yrs), 3.6 to 4.5 (8 yrs), and 4.0 to 5.0 tons ac^{-1} yr^{-1} (10 yrs), while that at Waseca ranged from 4.6 to 6.0 tons ac^{-1} yr^{-1} (7 yrs). The three best clones had 1.2 to 2.7 times greater biomass than controls throughout development of the 1995 Westport, 1997 Westport, and 2000 Waseca plantings. Genotype × environment interactions governed biomass production, with clone-mean rank correlations across sites ranging from 0.29 to 0.81. We identified both generalist genotypes (202.37, 5910100, D105, D124, NC14105) with elevated biomass across the region and specialist genotypes (220-5, 7300501, 80X01038, Crandon, NC13563) with exceptional biomass at specific locations.

KEY WORDS: hybrid poplar, tree improvement, productivity, clonal rank, genotype × environment interactions

*Corresponding author: U.S. Forest Service, Northern Research Station, 5985 Highway K, Rhinelander, WI 54501; Phone: (715) 362-1132; Email: rzalesny@fs.fed.us

VARIATION IN LATERAL AND BASAL ADVENTITIOUS ROOTING OF *POPULUS* IRRIGATED WITH LANDFILL LEACHATE: SELECTION OF FAVORABLE GENOTYPES FOR ENVIRONMENTAL BENEFITS

Ronald S. Zalesny, Jr.* and Jill A. Zalesny

U.S. Forest Service, Northern Research Station, Institute for Applied Ecosystem Studies

Successful establishment and productivity of short-rotation *Populus* crops depends upon adventitious rooting. Two common adventitious root types from *Populus* cuttings are: 1) *lateral roots* that develop from either preformed or induced primordia; and 2) *basal roots* that differentiate from callus at the base of the cutting in response to wounding. We irrigated 12 *Populus* clones (91.05.02, NC13460, NC13475, NC13680, NC14018, NC14104, NC14106, DM115, DN182, DN5, NM2, NM6) with municipal solid waste landfill leachate or well water (control) and evaluated root initiation (30 days after planting [DAP]) and root growth rate (45 DAP) among irrigation treatments, clones, and belowground portion of the cutting from which roots originated (upper, middle, lower laterals; basals). There were 3 (91.05.02) to 27 lateral roots (NC14018), with a mean of 16 roots, while the range for basal roots was 2 (91.05.02) to 10 roots (NC13680), with a mean of seven roots (44 percent of laterals). Leachate did not generally affect rooting across clones, root origins, and root types, but number of roots was greatest with leachate for NC13475 (40 percent greater than water) and NM2 (44 percent). The percent advantage of number of roots from the middle portion of the cutting relative to other sections was 120 percent (upper), 193 percent (lower), and 24 percent (basal). Overall, leachate did not affect root growth rate, while roots grew 1.5 to 3.4 cm day^{-1}, with a mean of 2.3 cm day^{-1}. Selecting *Populus* genotypes with lateral, basal, or both adventitious root types that thrive with leachate irrigation (i.e., NC13475, NM2) supports increased productivity potential of *Populus* feedstocks for fiber (pulp for paper), energy (cellulosics for ethanol, biomass for electricity), and environmental services (carbon sequestration, environmental remediation) necessary for long-term ecosystem sustainability.

KEY WORDS: phytotechnologies, forest genetics, tree improvement, hybrid poplar, adventitious root types

*Corresponding author: U.S. Forest Service, Northern Research Station, 5985 Highway K, Rhinelander, WI 54501; Phone: (715) 362-1132; Email: rzalesny@fs.fed.us

EVALUATION OF THE POTENTIAL OF HYBRID WILLOW AS A SUSTAINABLE BIOMASS ENERGY ALTERNATIVE CROP IN NORTHERN AND WEST-CENTRAL MINNESOTA

Diomides Zamora[a],*, Dean Current[b], and Mike Demchik[c]

[a]University of Minnesota Extension
[b]University of Minnesota - Center for Integrated Natural Resources and Agricultural Management
[c]University of Wisconsin - Stevens Point

Renewable sources of energy are becoming more important in Minnesota as the state is striving towards energy independence from fossil fuels. Woody biomass offers an important option for the production of biomass for energy particularly by the landowners in Minnesota. Short-rotation Woody Crops (SWRC), such as willow, provide both economic and ecological benefits, including erosion control, wildlife habitat enhancement, and carbon sequestration. This presentation will present the initial findings of our research on the potential of hybrid willow from New York as a sustainable biomass energy alternative crop in northern and western Minnesota. The willow varieties under investigation are *Salix discolor*, *Salix sachalinensis*, *Salix miyabeana*, and *Salix dasyclados*. Initial results showed that these varieties could survive in Minnesota despite harsher environmental growing conditions compared to New York. Survival and biomass production of these willow varieties were measured in 2007. Measurement will also be made in 2008. Survival of these varieties ranges from 74 to 91 percent. Initial results also showed that biomass production of each of the varieties is comparable with those plantings in New York and in southern Minnesota. Further, growth performance of willow varieties was found to be comparable to that of native willows in Minnesota. Results of this collective demonstration research will provide us guidance as to whether hybrid willows could be adopted in Minnesota as an alternative source of renewable energy while improving ecological sustainability and productivity.

KEY WORDS: hybrid willow, survival rate, biomass production

*Corresponding author: 322 Laurel St., Suite 21, Brainerd, MN 56401; Phone: (218) 828-2332; Email: zamor015@umn.edu

AUTHOR INDEX

Abahamson, Lawrence P. 1, 8, 54, 66

Alasia, Franco 40

Amidon, Thomas E. 66

Aneshansley, Daniel J. 1, 66

Arnold, R. Bruce 2

Aronsson, Pär 10, 41

Aubrey, Douglas 9

Aust, W. Michael 13

Baker, John 27

Banerjee, Sudipto 20

Bauer, Edmund O. 70

Bender, Bradford A. 36

Bentrup, Gary 3, 16

Berguson, William E. 4, 34, 72

Berndes, Göran 5, 55

Blazier, Michael A. 6, 29

Brown, John J. 7, 49

Bryan Jenkins 42

Buchholz, Thomas S. 8, 30

Buchman, Daniel J. 34

Cai, Haowen 20

Cameron, Kimberly D. 54, 66

Cobill, Robert 47

Coleman, Mark 9

Coyle, David R. 70

Current, Dean 16, 74

D'Amato, Anthony W. 11

David, Andrew J. 11

Demchik, Mike 74

Dimitriou, Ioannis 10

Domke, Grant M. 11

Doruska, Paul F. 57

Dosskey, Michael 3

Eaton, Jake 12

Eisenbies, Mark H. 13

Ek, Alan R. 11

Ficklin, Robert L. 58

Fore, Seth 14

Gopalakrishnan, Gayathri 15

Gordon, Andrew 16

Gordon, Gayle 42

Graham, Peter H. 31

Gray, Ed 42

Grünewald, Holger 17

Hafner, Sasha D. 45

Hale, Anna 47

Hall, Richard B. 18, 70, 72

Halvorsen, Kathleen E. 53

Hannon, Eugene R. 7

Hart, Quinn 42

Heissenbuttel, John 19

Jenkins, Bryan 42

Johnson, Gregg A. 20, 43, 66

Johnson, Jane M.F. 21

Johnson, Jon D. 22, 24, 56

Jung, Hans-Joachim G. 20, 43

Jurgens, Allan 23

Kallestad, Jeff C. 22, 24

Kantar, Michael 25

Kazaks, Hazen 26

Kelleher, Michael J. 8

Kittelson, Neal T. 7

Krueger, Erik 27

Labbé, Nicole 46

Labrecque, Michel 28

Lazarus, William 14

Leopold, Don J. 45

Levar, Thomas E. 34

Liechty, Hal O. 6, 29, 58

Luzadis, Valerie A. 30

Maclean, Ann L. 53

Maly, Craig C. 34

Mangan, Margaret E. 31

Mann, James 32

Marchand, Pierre P. 33

Masse, Sylvain 33

Maule, Rodrigo 55

McMahon, Bernard G. 34, 72

Meschke, Linda 35

Miller, Raymond O. 36

Mirck, Jaconette 37

Mitchell, Rob vii, 38, 64

Moore, Kenneth J. 39

Naber, Jeffrey D. 53

Nardin, Fabrizio 40

Neale, David B. 56

Negri, M. Cristina 15

Nelson, Richard 42

Nordh, Nils-Erik 41

Nowak, Chris A. 59

O'Brien, Timothy C. 34

Ochsner, Tyson 27

Ofezu, Godfrey J. 59

Ostry, Michael E. 63

Parker, Nathan 42

Patton-Mallory, Marcia 42

Pelkki, Matthew H. 6, 29, 51, 57, 58

Perlack, Robert D. 52, 68

Petersen, Katie B. 20, 43

Porter, Paul 14, 25, 27

Posselius, John 1, 66

Priepke, Ed 1

Pulley, Emily E. 44

Quaye, Amos K. 45

Rak, Dennis 66

Reicosky, Donald 27

Rials, Timothy G. 46

Ribic, Christine A. 50

Richard, Ed Jr. 47

Richardson, Jim vii, 48

Rodstrom, John R. 49

Rodstrom, R. Andrew 7, 49

Ruttens, Ann 69

Sample, David W. 50

Sarath, Gautam 64

Schirmer, Charles D. 45

Schmidt, Anneliese 42

Schoeneberger, Michele 3, 16

Schuler, Jamie L. 51

Seiler, John R. 13

Serapiglia, Michelle J. 54

Shamey, Anna M. 52

Sheaffer, Craig C. 20, 31, 43

Shonnard, David R. 53

Skog, Ken 42

Smart, Lawrence B. 1, 44, 54, 66

Snyder, Seth 15

Sparovek, Gerd 55

Spomer, Eric 66

Stanosz, Glen R. 72

Stanton, Brian J. 56

Stipanovic, Arthur J. 54

Stuhlinger, H. Christoph 51, 57

Sutherland, John W. 53

Tappe, Philip A. 6, 29, 58

Teodorescu, Traian Ion 28

Tew, Thomas 47

Tharakan, Pradeep J. 59

Thelemann, Ryan T. 20, 43

Thewys, Theo 69

Tiller, Kelly 60

Tittmann, Peter 42

Tschirner, Ulrike W. 20, 31, 43

Turhollow, Anthony F. 68

van Oosten, Cees ("Case") 61

Van Rees, Ken C. J. 62

Vance, Eric D. 13

Venette, Robert C. 63

Verwijst, Theo 41

Vogel, Kenneth 38, 64

Voigt, Tom 65

Volk, Timothy A. 1, 8, 30, 37, 45, 54, 59, 66

von Wühlisch, Georg 17

Walsh, Douglas B. 7

Wang, Michael 15

Ward, Kathleen M. 63

Weisberg, Sanford 31

Wells, Gary 3

West, Charles P. 6

White, Edwin H. 66

White, N. Larry 67

Wilkerson, Erin G. 68

Witters, Nele 69

Wright, Lynn L. 52

Wu, May 15

Wyse, Donald L. 31

Zalesny, Jill A. 70, 71, 72, 73

Zalesny, Ronald S. Jr. vii, 70, 71, 72, 73

Zamora, Diomides 74

Zhang, Qiong 53